HELP YOURSELF TO A JOB

HELP YOURSELF TO A

JOB

JACKIE LEWIS

Need2Know

PROFESSIONAL ADVICE & PRACTICAL HELP

© Jackie Lewis 1997

First published by Need2Know 1996
This edition published by Need2Know 1997
Need2Know, 1-2 Wainman Road, Woodston,
Peterborough PE2 7BU

Edited by Kerrie Pateman
Typesetting by Forward Press Ltd

Contents

Introduction

In these days of fierce competition, mass-marketing and high pressure sales, finding work is a full-time job in itself. Ways of getting a job are becoming more varied and sophisticated.

This book is not a guarantee to getting a job. Neither will it tell you 'you're the greatest thing since sliced bread', or 'you too can become a brain-surgeon in twelve short lessons'. This is a serious, no-nonsense look at the ways, means, and above all, the skills, necessary to find work.

It investigates the job market, and shows you how to assess your own skills and potential. It will show you how to present yourself in the best possible light - how to reduce your chance of being 'binned' before you get to the interview.

Early in 1997, the government cut funding for Employment Service courses for unemployed people by a third. Eligibility became more strict and the time allowed on courses became more limited. It is now more important than ever, therefore, to help yourself to a job. This book offers all the guidance you need to secure your way back into work. The courses, however, are still important because the facilities are free and they provide access to telephones, stamps and stationery. This book is designed to be used on its own or in conjunction with these courses. Follow my advice, make full use of their facilities and good luck!

If this book is of help - or there is an area you wish I had covered in more depth - I would love to hear from you. My advice in these pages is based on the experiences of my clients; without their feedback I could not have gained the courage to write these suggestions down. There is a wealth of information that simply had to be left out, so if you have a specific query or problem, I might still have the answer.

1 TAKING STOCK

- Courses can help
- Discovering skills and interests

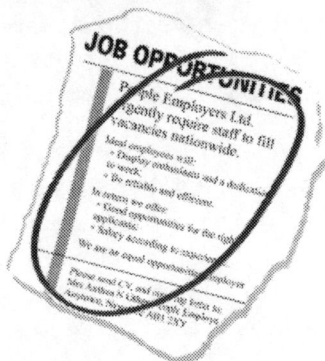

What are you looking for? Did you begin by looking for a repeat of what you had been doing in your last job; and then, as things became more and more desperate, resort to considering anything at all?

Sometimes unemployment gives you the chance to sit back and take a real look at your life; perhaps for the first time ever, because previously you were too busy earning the proverbial crust to have time to look at things. Also, there are other things you would have liked to pursue but simply didn't have the time. One of the ironies of working is that you have money but not the time. Now, of course, the coin has turned: money is the bugbear and time is on your hands.

Courses Can Help

Now that the worst has happened, wouldn't it make sense

to look at what is available? Many things are free or available at reduced cost to the unemployed. Almost all part-time college courses are free. A variety of training courses are available; expensive courses which, if you have a family to provide for, you wouldn't normally be able to indulge in, even if you could spare the time.

If you think it might take six to twelve months to find other employment, then it is worth-while to enrol on a course. Not only are you keeping yourself active, optimistic and in the mainstream, you are also topping up on skills, adding to your CV and networking - both of these latter items will be looked at in depth in succeeding chapters.

Courses do not have to be academic. If you are not 'bookish', or feel that you had enough of that in previous years, there are practical courses you could consider; carpentry, mechanics, dry-stone walling, hedge laying, conservation, lambing in spring. These are very expensive courses normally but most are free for those enrolling when in receipt of benefits. There are limits to the number of hours you can study without being considered 'unavailable for work' so it is best to check up on these at the benefits office.

There are courses specifically run by employment services for the unemployed which specialise in preparing people for work: from seminars which look at how to find, apply and interview for jobs, right through to organising retraining programmes for those who think the time has come for them to diversify.

Miners, for instance, have many skills, but no mines! There are many courses that they can go on and the sheer variety is endless. I know one ex-miner who said that the one thing he had enjoyed during his nearly thirty years in the pits, was gardening. He was divorced had no ties in the area, and was living with his parents, which he wanted to change. The answer was to obtain qualifications for which he undoubtedly had talent - gardening. He was offered a batch of interviews at stately homes with the National Trust; all of which came with a lodge or other 'idyllic' sounding accommodation. Perhaps he would now say that being made redundant was the best thing that ever happened to him.

Very often, people who have spent half their working life in high-powered, decision-making fields, have the same hankerings. When they are finally encouraged to sit back and assess what they would really like to do, the answer is that they would quite happily take a reduction in salary for a change of working life-style. Again, they too seem to hanker for the outdoors. Something more meandering - and somehow real - than the papers they have been signing for so many years.

Discovering Skills And Interests

So many people are stuck in jobs with no way out. People dare not give their jobs up when they have a mortgage and family to provide for. Once that worst nightmare has happened, there's no point in worrying about the next nightmare; now is the time to look around. Ask, enquire, consider options. But before you go to anyone else: ask yourself. That is the most important thing. Consider things you have not done before, find out about things you did not even know about.

If you have reached the stage of thinking you can't do anything, have no skills left, perhaps because you have been out of work for so long; then try a simple test on yourself.

- With a clean piece of paper, list every job you have ever had - every single one, no matter how short a time you might have worked there.

- Next, break down each of those jobs into their component parts: was there machinery; did you serve customers; did you handle money; stock orders; did you carry heavy weights; did you train any staff; work long hours?

- List everything: every single, smallest thing you can think of.

The result of this is, firstly, you will surprise yourself at just how long the list is. But the next step can be even more profitable.

- Now list all the hobbies and skills you have in your none-working life. *Gardening? Fellwalking? Antiques? Football?*

  List them all, even if they were only fads. You want them on that piece of paper. List the aspects of them.

  With the two breakdown lists you can now work out a pattern by ticking those you were especially good at and those you were bad at. Those you loved and those you hated.

Perhaps you dealt with customers and you think you were particularly good at that. Perhaps you had trouble with the boss who thought you spent too much time on the customers and not enough on the stock control. In another job, you were good at helping the new lad who started on the job, but, again, had problems with the petty rules of the factory.

In your hobbies, perhaps the one thing you really love is driving - long journeys? Your first instinct might be to say, 'but everyone likes driving!' No. Some people do it because they have to, or it makes their life easier. Not everyone loves to drive - and if you think it is one of the things you do best...

The result of this, from just two jobs and one hobby, is that this person is not keen on petty rules or rigid systems. He is 'people oriented' and will therefore want to put them first, no matter what the boss says. In the wrong job, this will lead him into trouble - or dismissal - but in the right job it will be prized and could earn him a lot of money. If he always has trouble with the boss, it doesn't necessarily mean he's a trouble-maker. More often it means that he is working at a level that is too low for him.

The list I've just invented is a classic example of someone who - for his own sake and interests - should be in some kind of retail or sales management. Something where he can be his own boss, can help people, take pride in providing a good service and can delegate.

Just as easily, depending on how strong the desire to drive is - this person would enjoy driving for a living; the isolation, being away from the boss, having most of the decision-making left to himself - so what about area-sales-management?

One thing is for sure; if you enjoy something you are probably good at it. If you don't like something, better to stand aside and let someone else get on with it; because to force yourself to continue is depressing, at best.

Too often to count are the times that I have looked over someone's lists, found suitable jobs and asked if they've ever considered them, and been told; 'I've always wanted to do that!' They stare at me as though suspecting I've just read their palms or tea-leaves but the answers are there clearly in their own writing. They just haven't had time to sit back and contemplate before.

If you have never tried this, then make yourself a drink, sit back and do it now. Don't rush it, but at the same time, don't turn it into hard work. Just jot down the words.

This is only a 'taster' offered as an exercise to start you thinking about yourself with more precision and confidence.

Later, we shall go into this aspect in depth and you will see just what a positive affect it has on your confidence and attitudes.

2 BE PREPARED

- The planning is all
- Are you in a special category?

No matter how desperate you are at this moment; for a job, for income, for self-esteem, don't rush out and start searching for work. It will be self-defeating. Ask yourself some questions first. *Are you prepared?*

I almost never come across anyone who can answer yes to that question; and those who do are usually mistaken.

The very basics then. *Can you lay your hands, immediately, on the following?*

- Stamps
- Telephone
- Stationery
- CVs
- Yellow pages for all your neighbouring regions
- A COICS book
- A KOMPAS book
- A Thompsons Directory

- Vehicle
- Travelling Expenses
- Personal fallback for children, pets, house
- A cleaned interview suit, accessories
- Do you know exactly what to say and do at initial contact, interview, speculative visit?

Above all, can you say 'yes' to all these things, every day? If you said no to any of these things, then you are not prepared.

One of the courses I run lasts for a month. It is for people who have been out of work for a year or longer. It takes the first week just to convince them that there is hope. Another half a week at least to capture their interest and a resurgence of self-motivation. Only by the end of the second week are they confident with their letters, CVs and form-filling. It takes the whole four weeks for them to prepare for the interviews; and by then they are enthusiastic, confident and - above all - fully prepared.

The Planning Is All

The simple fact is, the more preparation you put in, the better your success will be. Don't leave any areas unattended; make sure that you have dealt with all the practical issues and then look at personal ones. If you have been out of work for a long time, for instance, how will your routine be affected?

Expect the unexpected

Your lifestyle has to be turned on its head when you return to work. If you are a single parent, have you arranged for childminding? If you have pets, will there be a problem with them suddenly being left alone all day?

Many people do run successful careers with these private commitments, so they are not insurmountable problems; but you do need to prepare yourself in advance.

If you are a man with a family, how much have you been doing at home during your time off work? This can cause a real shift in chores and responsibility.

If you are a woman, do you have family support? Not just family 'lip-service'; do they really support you - do they do their full percentage share of the housework (ie not only washing the dishes, but who cleans the toilet?), the shopping, the planning?

Make no mistake about this; whoever you are, whatever your circumstances, when you get your new job it will almost certainly be at short notice; and in the first weeks back at work you are going to be shattered! You won't have the energy to eat your dinner let alone cook everyone else's, and go and fetch it first!

The Benefits Trap

If you have been unemployed for a long time, can you afford your first weeks at work? Are you caught in the *Benefit Trap*? Will you be able to find the money to get to work? If you receive your letter on Friday telling you that you have got the job, they will probably ask you to start on

Monday. Can you sort everything out in that time? Perhaps you can post a letter to the Job Centre to 'sign off' but that won't give you time to sort out other things. What about your housing benefit, mortgage repayments, council tax? You can see a claimants advisor at your local benefits office now who will give you an estimate of what to expect when you return to work. They will also advise you on what to do if you find work at short notice. Remember; they are on your side; they want you to succeed and they will be happy to offer any help they can.

None of these problems are insurmountable - no one problem is even a difficult one. The trouble begins if you have ignored them, allowed them to pile up; then you will arrive at work on your first day with an extra workload: worries about how you are going to handle everything.

Think now not later

Clear-headedness is an important factor of success in job searching. Perhaps the most important factor of all. Decide what you want, how to go about it, develop a plan of action, research the job market, find your own strengths and weaknesses: use every weapon at your disposal.

Bills and debt

Turn every weakness into something positive. If you are unemployed then resist paying for anything. You don't need to pay for stationery, phone calls, long-distance travel to interviews. You don't need to search for work from your own home, being isolated, using your own heating, electricity, coffee. There's an office in town, at your disposal; use it. I have used Job Club three times when I have been out of work. If I lose my job tomorrow, I will be back at Job Club on Monday.

Are You In A Special Category?

If you have a disability then *use it to your advantage*. The government offers extra help for special needs categories; make the most of anything that is offered. Once you have got your job you can prove yourself. If anything offers you a head start, take it.

Ex-offenders

If you are in this category and you think you will never work again and can only envisage a downward spiral into poverty or re-offending then please believe this: *I have had many ex-offenders on my client list: they have all found work.*

You need extra help with your CV from someone who understands the legalities and concepts of 'spent convictions' - and you need realistic advice on how to make your applications. Don't lie; believe it or not, you have many qualities which are attractive to employers so you need to handle your past in a way which does not raise fears or prejudices.

If you are still serving a prison sentence as you read this, then you probably have access to a course to help you find work. If not, and you really do want to make a fresh start, write to me at the address in this book.

Age

If you think age is a barrier to you finding work, you can use that to your advantage too; there are companies that specifically prefer older age groups. Your Job Centre knows who they are, have you asked them?

Younger people can come up against even worse age barriers than the older groups now. People are reaching their twenties who can say that they have *never* had a job. This has to be a first in British history. Employment Services now offers a course (called *Workwise*) for the eighteen to twenty-four age group which specialises in those people. Again, take advantage of it. They are expensive courses under normal circumstances.

Women

If you are a woman who can fit into the 'Women Returners' category, please look at what is available in your area. I went on a 'Women into Management' course run by Staffordshire University. I cannot recommend this course highly enough, or the woman who ran it. The elements of the course were almost identical to the one I run, but it is specifically aimed at women and does an immense amount to boost your confidence. As far as I am aware, the only factor which decides your eligibility is that you are unemployed and would like to return to work.

I would also suggest you read the book, *Women Returners* by Linda Stokes to see what is relevant to your area.

3 APPEARANCE MATTERS

- Get the exercise 'high'
- Dress for success

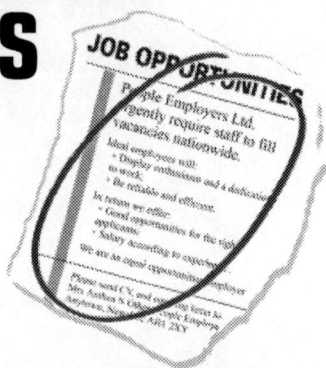

How do you feel today? If you have been unemployed for a while, are you feeling slightly depressed - or very depressed? Are you a little run down? I would guess that only one in twenty people turn up to my courses looking as though they are fit, healthy and prepared for a new career. The reason could be that they still consider there is nothing to prepare themselves for, nothing worth getting 'dressed to kill' for. But it is more likely that they are lethargic and depressed because of excessive financial pressure.

Get The Exercise 'High'

I'm not going to lecture about exercise because I know at first hand that nothing anyone says or does will make you visit a gym if you don't want to. However, as one who did once 'partake', it shames me to write this section because I know how well I felt when I trained regularly; better than I've ever felt in the whole of my adult life. Exercise really does affect your mental well-being.

Dress For Success

Do as much or as little as you can afford in this area; but what you can't afford in cash, make up for in time. Are your clothes presentable? Are you presenting the right image? If you want a management position, there is no point slouching around in a track suit. You need your suit; is it clean, pressed, tidy? Do you have everything to go with it?

There are definite styles and standards of dress according to one's 'position' in society - whether we like it or not. It is a factor and therefore pointless complaining that you cannot pass an interview for a Conservative party spokesman if you dress like a punk rocker! Even without these extremes there is still a code of dress which is both more subtle and more distinctive and it does not necessarily mean that you have to abandon your own style completely.

We all complain about prejudice and yet we all practise it at some level. Simply sit in a town square and watch people passing. Estimate their income, their lifestyle, their careers; we all do it and we make these judgements according to their clothes, their haircut, their age and shape. A teacher dresses differently to a bank manager. A company director differently again. And yet, the Head of a secondary school doesn't dress like a teacher... that person tends to dress more like the company director - suits again, instead of the casual slacks or flowing skirt. Why is this? It comes down to the command for respect again.

Whatever the reason, take note of the clothes worn by the bracket you are aiming for and ignore it at your peril. Even if the company accepts you, you yourself will feel out of place if you do not 'blend in' with the others and life can be made difficult enough in a new position without adding to it.

It is a complicated subject to go into in any depth. Without going into the argument of whether or not we should allow ourselves to get dragged into such shallow value-judgements. If you are ambitious, however, you are probably a part of that system anyway and would want to take any step to accomplish your aim.

If this is the case, firstly, take a lot of notice of the area in which you live and want to work - fashions change according to where you reside. Secondly, dress for the income bracket you are heading for - not the bracket you are in right now (that dirty word, poverty again!)

For men a suit or a good blazer is still a prerequisite to

interviews and for women it can be even more complex. It depends on the amount of respect you want to command; if you want to be taken seriously then make sure that you are wearing the clothes and not them wearing you. Choose muted colours without fancy patterning or cut and a pair of court shoes.

You do not need to be in the height of fashion to make a good impression. In fact, I would think that it would probably work against you to be too fashionable in any work other than that directly linked to the fashion industry. Nor do you need to go into ten year's debt on your plastic to look good.

Clothes which are smart are not necessarily expensive, nor do they need to be new. In fact, it can be much better for you to stick to what you already have for an interview, because the 'comfort factor' is very important in a situation which can be nerve-racking.

I would say that 'quietness' wins every time. Make sure you choose something that is a distinctive colour but dark or subdued. A navy or grey suit for men and those colours or black for women. A plain white or ivory shirt or blouse and no fancy jewellery for men or women.

Briefcases are now standard uniform for women in business. One word of warning; watch the weight, for many briefcases are illogically heavy when empty. If you have to carry a lot of paperwork and files each day, it can be a hassle.

A handbag isn't necessary unless your briefcase is so unwieldy it takes half an hour to find your keys each time you want them; but choose your briefcase with this in mind.

4 WHERE TO GET HELP

- Decisions, decisions

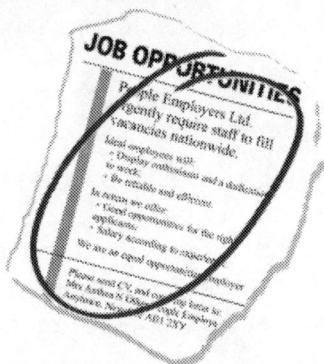

Employment Services offer a variety of courses lasting various lengths. They show you options which are available and offer facilities to find out about other options.

One of the benefits of these courses is that the course leaders are skilled in showing you how to assess your own skills. They have no axe to grind, they are completely independent of Employment Services or any other official body.

Job Centre

To go on one of these courses you simply go along to the Job Centre. They will enrol you on the next available course; usually within a month. When you get there you will be asked to list all your skills. These do not have to be skills you have learned at work. Anything which you think you do well, that you enjoy - gardening, for instance.

It is amazing how many skills show themselves, which you had not previously considered in relation to work. Many times, what shows is that the work you have previously been doing is not necessarily what you would have been best at. But you had not been through a controlled assessment before you applied for that job.

Computers

You will have access to computers which have programs to assess your talents according to your stated likes and dislikes. Along with your qualifications, and willingness or otherwise to retrain, this allows the computer to deliver an astonishingly accurate profile for you to consider.

Universities and colleges

This is not the only way to assess yourself; there are other organisations which now offer very similar courses; perhaps your local University. It is always worth calling your nearest colleges to see what they have to offer; better still, call in and ask. They are all worth looking into.

Local libraries

Even if you are not a regular visitor to your local library, now is the time to become one. Firstly, all local council vacancies will be held there. Secondly, check out their notice boards for anything that might be relevant to you. Don't just look at one section on the shelves for quite often the books of interest to you might be scattered over several subject areas. On my last visit, I found books on 'How to write a CV' in the 'Business Management' section. In the other library in town, that same subject was housed in the

'Self-help' section.

Job Club

What if you cannot afford to make dozens of enquiries? That is even simpler. Job Club is the answer and is free for the asking. You do not have to use it specifically to find paid work. It can be used to search for a course, career information, as well as employment. At Job Club, all your stationery, postage and telephone calls are free. And the support from the other people attending has a large upsurge on morale.

Careers Service

If you thought that this service was for school-leavers then think again. It was a careers officer who first set me on the road to University as a mature student. These people can be very good. However, I was told recently that they have started to charge for their services; but again, it will undoubtedly be free to the unemployed.

Careers analysis

This really is the deluxe end of the market! Costing around £200 - £300 for one day, it is an investment that takes thought and commitment. I have to admit, I would take the plunge if I could afford it and the assessments are usually carried out by psychologists who specialise in this area. They claim to be able to assess precisely what your talents are down to the 'nth' degree. I say 'claim' not to be derogatory, but because I have no first-hand experience of them. If I were planning a career in business and wanted to climb the ladder in terms of promotion, then I would certainly take one of these assessment programmes. I suspect that the initial outlay would be more than repaid by the increased earning potential. There are contact addresses at the back; but please do your homework because I have very little knowledge of this area.

Decisions, Decisions...

- *First Step* Think about what you would like to do. Have some ideas of your own but don't close any doors at this stage; the objective is to open even more.

- *Second* Go along to Job Centre, the library, and perhaps your local colleges of further education. Look at their leaflets and see what is available, what is relevant to you.

- Do you have a CV? Is it up-to-date? Do you know what the latest CVs look like? If the answer is no to any one of these questions, then consider one of the courses on offer; either Job Plan, Job Club, Job Search Seminar or Executive Job Club.

These days, whatever your aim and prospects, you do need a Curriculum Vitae. And they are expensive. On these courses they will be provided, to your own specifications, with as much or as little assistance as you require, free.

If, after reading the dozens of leaflets in the Job Centre, you still have no clear idea of what you want then I would strongly recommend that you take one of these courses. They will open your mind to many options you have perhaps not even heard of and you will be under no obligation to follow any of the suggestions. Neither do they pressurise you into looking for work specifically; because it could well be that the way forward for you is to retrain.

Final word: Don't limit your options to just one of these sources. *They are all available - why not use them all?*

5 THE HIDDEN JOB MARKET

- Speculative applications
- Networking

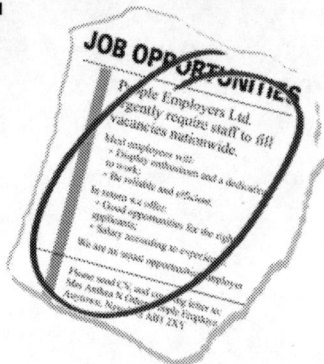

Where do you look for work - newspapers, Job Centres, specialist magazines? Only about a quarter of all vacancies are filled in this way, and what an arena to put yourself in. For each job that is advertised, anything up to hundreds of letters of application arrive. Many jobs that are advertised in newspapers have already gone before you even see them. Some companies have advertised internally but are required by law to advertise outside also. In these circumstances, the result is often a foregone conclusion.

Speculative Applications

Whilst writing this paragraph, I picked up a local newspaper at random, and turned to the 'Sits Vac' page. Twelve vacancies. The newspaper covers three towns and only twelve businesses have advertised with them. I know for a fact that there are over a thousand vacancies currently in this area.

A good seventy-five percent of the vacancies are not advertised. An employer has a filing cabinet full of applications; if he gets a vacancy he can write to those people. He saves hundreds of pounds on advertising and many man-hours sifting through applications and CVs.

It is far cheaper and easier for him to do this. It is cheaper and easier for you to do this too. It is called *speculative applying*. You send a letter to a prospective employer. You imagine it will be instantly binned if there is no immediate vacancy. This happens far less often than you might think. Any employer with foresight will have a special file for these applications. If your letter looks interesting, that's where it will go. There is one other factor to consider with speculative applications too; *you are the only contender.*

Networking

Someone resigns. When they do so, they tell their employer they know of someone who is keen and able. The employer likes this person, is sorry they are leaving; trusts their judgement. He says to tell the friend to come along for interviewing. This is called *networking*. There are many ways of networking. And they are all effective.

I know of a company right now which has vacancies. They have not advertised externally, they are not interviewing. They have put a sign up in their staff canteen asking if anyone has a friend who wants a job. They are fed up of interviewing and hiring unsuitable people. They believe that if it is a friend of a present employee, they will know exactly what the terms and conditions are from the friend and therefore be willing and able before they start. They believe that the present employee will not recommend anyone unsuitable because they themselves will have to work with them. *Have you told all your friends that you are looking for work?* This too, is called networking.

You read your local free paper. There is an article of a local company securing a large foreign contract. There is a photo of a smiling happy company director, well pleased with his success. A new contract means more work; which means more men; which means he'll need to advertise soon - unless you write to him first. And you won't be in competition with two or three hundred other people who respond to his advertisement. This is networking - and initiative.

Are you good at talking to strangers? Good on the telephone? Have you tried calling up employers? They are far friendlier than you might imagine. This is like *cold calling*. If the very thought of it sends shivers down your spine, then don't try it; *but it does work* - I see people get jobs in this way during *every* week of my work, and some people are 'natural' at it; they prefer this method and it shows in their voices.

Are you good at face to face meetings? Have you tried calling on a company on spec? Again, I have seen this work. I have used this method myself and it has worked for me.

Finally, *are you on first name terms at your local job centre?* Why not? Do you think they are the enemy? When I was depressed, demoralised, unemployed- I felt that way.

I couldn't have been more wrong. One day I walked in to their office, stood looking at the board and an advisor came up to me.

'I've been looking out for you,' she said, 'A vacancy has come in; perfect for you, and it hasn't even gone on the board yet.' They genuinely want to help; but they know what people think of them and it's hard pushing yourself forward in that situation - isn't it?

6 THE NUMBERS GAME

- More is more
- Check your feedback

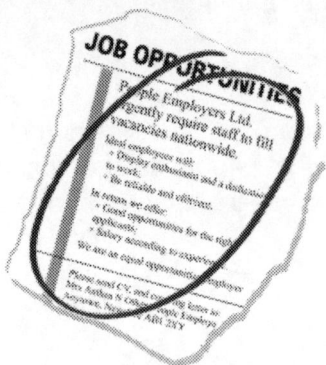

More Is More

No one way of looking for work is right; not all methods are right for everyone. But *use every method there is*. This is the numbers game, and the more shots you fire, the more chance you have of hitting your target.

Tell yourself the truth now. How many jobs have you applied for this week. Any? A few? Have you sent off twenty letters of application today? One thing is sure; the longer you have been out of work, the fewer applications you will be sending out.

If you began reading this book because you are working out your notice with a company, or have only just left, then you are very lucky. The longer you are out of work the more difficult it becomes for you to find your way back into it. Use this time now; don't sit back and relax for a few months because you will be building up problems for yourself.

Whatever your circumstances, the simple facts are these: you won't get a job without making the approaches; and *you lessen your chances by not making the right approaches - in the right way.*

Check Your Feedback

As an example (one which I see regularly); if you sent out twenty applications last week and you have not had a single reply, that is *not* because there were no vacancies. It was because there was something wrong with your letter. If you only sent out two or three then that could be a possible reason, but not with so many letters. So, what was wrong? Your letter itself could have been badly written, badly presented. Was it written on lined 'corner shop' paper? That's your problem then. An easy one to resolve.

But if it wasn't - if you're sure there was nothing wrong with the paper, the writing, the wording? Then there's something wrong with the content. Perhaps you have targeted wrongly.

If you send out a lot of letters and you get your required interviews - but then hear no more, then there's something wrong with your interview technique.

The feedback is the answer - if you get none, you have a problem with what you are offering because, by sheer definition of numbers, if you put out enough feelers then you *must* get a response. Don't underestimate the power of a sympathetic rejection. Every week I have clients who are pleased, spurred on, by the letters they receive - *apologising for not being able to offer them a job!*

These are not pathetic wretches who are easily pleased; they are people who have worked hard to master the techniques of job hunting and who, for the first time for many, are receiving feedback to their letters. Last week they wrote for jobs and didn't even get a reply; this week they wrote letters based on what they have learnt and have had a forty-per-cent reply; *that is progress.* Next week?

And just in case your thoughts are; 'Ah! But do any of her clients get jobs?' They do indeed. If they want a job: *they get a job!* And if they want to diversify, that's what I help them to do. Retrain? Yes. Back to school; brilliant, that's my favourite challenge.

When I say 'fire as many shots as you can', I do not mean for you to apply for any and every vacancy you see. You must have a target in the first place and in this respect, I think the fewer targets you have, the better. Decide what you want and then aim for it. If you simply want any job - unskilled factory work - then you can still pin it down further. The more precisely you target, the better will be your chances. *Single-mindedness always wins.*

Once you have decided what kind of work you are aiming for, then you can start sending out mass applications.

One of my clients was a young girl who had left school a couple of years previously and had only had odd jobs as casual shop-assistant. When she first arrived she said she wanted 'anything'. After a week she said she had always wanted to be a hairdresser. 'Have you applied to any?' I asked.

'No, they always want experience.'

'Would you be prepared to train?'

'Oh, yes, I'd like that.'

'Without money?'

'I'm without money now.'

'Have you thought of offering your services free, in exchange for the training?'

I suggested she contact her local colleges to ask what they would require from her. They told her that they would train her on day-release if she could secure a place for herself at a salon.

I contacted the government training companies who said they would monitor her, ensure she got a 'fair deal' and her examinations and would pay all her expenses - again, if she could secure for herself a salon and a college course.

By then - half way through week two - she had looked at the techniques of letter writing, interviews, speculative phone calls and her CV had been completed. She was very shy and didn't want to touch the telephone, so we concentrated on compiling a good letter to accompany her CV.

The first thing was, she did have experience - a hairdressing salon is still a shop; there would be customers, money, a till, stock. She pointed this out in her letter and ensured that her referees would back her up.

When this was done, we targeted all the salons in her immediate area using her local Yellow Pages. The first batch of letters went out on Thursday evening, and a second batch went out Friday.

I warned her to be patient - we hadn't completed the 'A's yet - and I felt very sorry for her, painstakingly writing letter after letter in her 'best handwriting', for hours on end.

When we met again the following Monday morning she told me she had received a letter from one of the salons on the Saturday. She telephoned (!) and went in for an interview the same day. The manager immediately offered her the placement. That Monday, the college offered her the training and a placement officer set her expenses and so on in operation.

The girl had been out of work for two years and yet within ten days of setting a realistic target she was embarked on a career.

7 TOWARDS A CV

- Define your skills
- Personal qualities
- Achievements
- Work experience, qualifications, career history
- Use these words!

You now have to get to know yourself. You do this in order to decide what kind of work you would like to do. Then you have to do it again, this time in order to decide how best to present yourself. This will take you from whatever point in your life you have reached. Whether you have already decided what you want to do, you are already employed and want to change/diversify, or you are unemployed and want to secure work for yourself in the shortest possible time. This chapter will prepare your mind for what is ahead, and result in the CV that you can send out with pride.

What you put on your CV that will show you, your personality, succinctly without either lying or wasting space. And in order to do this, you have to know yourself, and perhaps learn to see yourself in a new light. This is no time for personal put-downs or shyness! Accurate self-assessment is required here without either boasting or holding back.

You need to look at four areas of your life:

- Skills
- Achievements
- Personal Qualities
- Personal Interests

First of all, define your basic skills because these will lead you into the other areas;

- If you have a driving licence, for instance.
- If you are a very organised person, or a good time-keeper.
- You might think that 'anyone can do these things'; but they can't. Some people cannot get up in the morning with three alarm clocks strapped to their head (as my household will testify!) and some people are simply not organised. These are skills which not everyone shares or to the same degree.
- They are positive attributes simply by definition that not everyone shares them.

When I employed people, I looked for people who shared the same personal values (that is, I looked for people I liked) and then I looked for qualities which they had and I lacked; qualities that would complement the team. And for this I looked for people who were very organised in the small details - which I lacked - or who could concentrate on seemingly unimportant aspects of the job - which I didn't have time for. This, to me, meant that all aspects of the business were being enhanced and I could concentrate my attention on the area in which I excelled - planning and developing the business.

So don't only list those skills which are obviously work-orientated either; remember from previous chapters that your personal interests are where most clues are to be gathered. Many of these skills are transferable. Perhaps you created your garden out of a wilderness. 'It's just a garden, nothing fancy.' Is it? Didn't it show good planning, foresight, perseverance, hard work, a creative eye, faith in yourself, good judgement of conditions... Need I go on?

When you have done this, list the ways each of these skills could be applied to the work place - if you have already used the same skills at work, so much the better, but you don't have to have done so. *List how you could use them* - these are the transferrable skills.

Now, some of these skills are valuable to you - you have a supporting nature, a lot of common sense, and so on. Some of these skills might be very valuable for an employer too.

Which, of the ones you have listed *will be of most value to an employer*? Remember: *your skills are the product which he will buy and you want to sell.*

And which of them give most satisfaction to you?

You will have two separate lists here and some skills will be repeated on both. Don't worry if you seem to be listing too many things; the more you list, the longer you spend looking at yourself, the better it will be. And if you are still looking at a page that is virtually blank except for one or two words, don't worry. Just keep going, you will find this is simply because you are not used to doing such exercises.

A point will come when everything fits into place and you will be able to start writing.

Don't give up at this stage: it really is important that you do this for yourself.

If you go on a course, although the leaders will help you, they will not pressurise you into working on your skills. They could not pressurise you no matter how much a disservice they might think you are doing to yourself. And with the numbers in the group they don't have the time to give you the hours of help you might need. *Be independent on this - no one knows you as well as you do yourself.* A course leader will help you to compile a CV based on the *information you offer*. It is better for all concerned, therefore, if you work on your own skills, defining and streamlining them, yourself. It only takes a few minutes to jot down these notes - what takes longer is the thought-process.

This is what you don't have time for in the group situation and which you should do at home away from interruption.

On such a course you will be given help within the context of the group and it might be suggested that you all work on it at home.

I rarely find anyone who does so; they treat it almost as though it is 'back to school' and homework. In my role as leader, I cannot then ask them to work harder, do more to help themselves; I can only pass the skills sheet on to be compiled into a CV. I don't think that anyone can compile a CV which does justice to themselves in one day. Even someone who is skilled at writing CVs - I spend *every* working day with them, yet I couldn't make one for myself in such a short time. If you were to ask me for a rough guess as to how long you should spend, I would say a week, minimum. Not just writing for that is the easy part, but *thinking, analysing, checking over the facts - reading up on the subject.*

I cannot assert this strongly enough; *the more time you put into this now, the more profitable it will be for you in the future.*

You have compiled your two lists which comprise your *basic skills*. Now it is time to look at your *specific skills*. Again, these do not have to be things you have done at work. I have written articles which have been published; I did not do that at work yet I would be a fool not to include it in a CV. If you cannot visualise how to do this, a good way of looking at it is in terms of results which have followed on from your basic skills.

- I like writing. That is a basic skill. The specific skills which come from that are that I can type; I can use a word-processor; I can research material; analyse documents and reports; maintain a filling system; and so on. I could make this list a lot longer - *You should do the same.*

If your lists seem to be growing and shooting off in all directions at this stage, again this is better for you. You can always develop patterns and order later; the important thing for now is to get it all down. You will surprise yourself with how many skills you have and that can only be good for your confidence. I would say don't even think of stopping until you have filled a good four sheets of A4 paper!

Shaping and editing

This process will have opened your mind to your own abilities. Now you can begin to edit them. Looking through, you will see that some skills are much more pronounced than others. You can say, 'I'm a good team member' but then you think 'Yes, but I don't always like to be surrounded by people'- now you are getting to know yourself; not only what you are good at but what you *like being good at.*

Personal interests

If you break down your personal interests in exactly the same way as you have done with your skills, you should come up with another skills list. This one is very important for two reasons. Firstly, your personal interests are those things you like doing best. So far, you might have worked for the money you get in return; but hobbies you tend to have to pay for! If it's cooking, you have to buy the ingredients, the tools, the supply of gas, etc. If it's body building, you buy the use of facilities, the vitamins, the extra food, you endure pain, and so on.

Secondly, whatever you are particularly interested in, you are almost certainly very good at. By this, I don't mean those things you do now and then just because someone drags you along to it. A reluctant squash player is not usually a good one. What would you get up for at five a.m. for? What would you give up smoking for? Perhaps you don't always or even often do it now, simply because you can no longer afford to - horse riding, karting, windsurfing are expensive hobbies if you are unemployed and have young children to feed and clothe. But would you be doing it every day if you had the money or facilities?

List all these interests; and then list all the skills involved.

Example

- Horse riding

  You are fit, strong, healthy. You like animals. Know about animal husbandry, nutrition, safety. You are brave, take calculated risks, can handle threatening behaviour. You can train - yourself and animals - can face and endure possible injury. You like the outdoors, all weathers... Perhaps also you like the competitive element of eventing or showing; that, then, will incorporate another list of skills. It goes on.

If you have several hobbies and interests and you list them all in this way, keep asking yourself why you like them, what aspects; the first thing you will begin to notice is how many of these skills repeat themselves. And they are the important ones; the essential ingredients which characterise you.

Personal Qualities

Perhaps the previous lists have already led you to this section; you already have a mental list of several qualities. On courses we offer lists for people to work from. The list is not very long and we suggest that members tick off those qualities which apply to them, stroke through those which definitely don't and then add some more. People never seem to add more. I suspect the reason for this is that they are so busy following our guidelines and suggestions that they have switched their brain into a 'follow instructions' mode and are unable then to switch back to their own thinking.

So bear this in mind as you look through the following prompt list; you do yourself no service to simply follow my list without adding your own. Use the thesaurus; check out other books on the subject, what they have listed, think up your own. Better still, work out your own list of personal qualities first and then use mine to add to it.

- Hopefully you will have at least forty or fifty qualities listed.
- Now choose from these a maximum of ten which in your view 'sums you up'.
- And of those, highlight half.

All of these words should be in your CV, but the final four or five should be incorporated into one powerful sentence.

Achievements

Too many times to begin to count, I ask people what achievement they have made and they say none, or can't think. As the week progresses things pop up in conversation and I stop them and say; 'Did you put that in your CV?' The answer is invariably no.

A recent client represented the country in a field sport but it was never mentioned as we went through skills, nor did he write it down - he had forgotten! When I questioned him on this, it turned out that there were several other areas of sport that he had excelled in, none of which he had mentioned. He pointed to one of his co-members and said 'Well, what about him; he was a professional boxer!' This second person, presumably to deflect my astonishment, pointed to a third person and said; 'Well *he* manages a football team!' I asked them all why they hadn't listed these things and they said, 'They weren't work and they weren't hobbies.' What were they then? Sport. They are skills, achievements, *things to be proud of!*

List them. If you taught your kid sister to read *list it.* If you dragged someone out of the river when they had cramp; *list it.* It doesn't matter what category they come under; *it is your achievement so list it.*

This section differs from previous ones in that, before, you were listing ideas, qualities about yourself, likes and dislikes. Now you are onto more concrete aspects: *things you have actually learned.*

- Don't concentrate on things you have achieved only recently; go back to school days.

- List everything. It doesn't have to be something you did particularly well either: you didn't have to come first in the relay; you took part.

- It could be that you made a pretty mediocre job of something; but you learned from it, and you know you would do better next time.

- Perhaps you went into something and realised partway through that though you liked some aspects, there were others you just weren't suited to; *list it and list the aspects you liked and didn't like.* You have learned something about yourself in that and, where you have realised there were required skills that you couldn't perform, so too there were skills that you could.

But your achievements don't end there.

- What about examinations?
- Have you been on any training or retraining courses?
- Did you go on to further education? University?
- Do you speak another language?
- Have you taught people to ride horses, to drive, to ride a motorcycle?
- Do you have your Lifesavers certificate?

Any kind of qualification goes here; any kind of training course, any group you belong to. Don't worry if they don't seem to fit into this category; you have an HND in mechanics and you are a member of a local poetry society - it doesn't matter at this stage as it can all be tidied up later. The important thing is to write everything down because if you don't, you'll forget.

Now in all these hundreds of sheets of A4 paper which you have filled in and scattered over table, settee and floor, which are the most important skills, qualities and qualifications - *which are worth most to a prospective employer?*

If you already know exactly what kind of work you are going to target, this exercise will be easier for you. If you don't know, leave yourself some room to manoeuvre.

Keep the sheets, because as we move on you will almost certainly become so enthusiastic about a particular type of work that you will start to target it. And then you might want to review your lists - without having to spend days compiling them again!

Of all the lists you have so far compiled, make up one shortlist for each. (Now you can start being a bit tidier too.) Keep each category down to around ten or a dozen items. Of these final choices, try to grade them according to how important they are - to you and to an employer - and to how relevant you think they'll be to your future work.

At this point do try to think if there is anything you might have left out. It is always worth looking through related books, backtracking - or one last flick through the Thesaurus.

Work Experience, Qualifications, Career History

If you have persevered through all the previous exercises, this next bit should be easy. This is the stage of 'names, dates, times, and reasons' - your alibi, or so it often feels. I wonder why we feel we are being interrogated when we compile our CVs or, later, when we prepare for interview? I guess because we are essentially private people and questions from strangers seem intrusive.

Whatever the reasons, it has to be done and this is the stage you have reached. If you already have a CV, the work should be easier. What you need to do now is list, chronologically, all education, all training, and all of your work history to date.

Don't worry if you've had fifty jobs in the last twenty years; this is still only for your use. The main thing right now is to get it all down so that you can see a pattern and know what to use and what to discard. In a CV you must not leave blank spaces, unanswered questions. If you work from a sheet that already has blanks then it can only get worse.

If you have had a long and varied work history this cannot be done in five minutes. Just sigh and get on with it - you'll be glad you did when it's over!

So for each item on your list:

✿ *Example - Secondary school*
    You need the name and address of the school, the years you attended, and any exams you sat, the subjects and grades. Any achievements can be listed here too; team captain, school prefect, whatever - even if it was thirty years ago; it still reminds you of how good you were!
✿ *Example - College of Further Education*
    You need the dates, the name and address, the subjects studied and the grades. You might not need all this information but you won't be able to decide without it.
✿ *Example - Work History*
    For each job you need the dates (start and finish), the name and address of employer, the job you did and your reason for leaving. At the end of this, everything from secondary school onwards should be laid out in front of you.

This could be half a page to ten pages depending on your age and how many jobs you have had. At the end of it, it will show you what kind of CV you need.

Say you have had three jobs, all in a similar line of work but which shows progression in each one; you haven't been fired and your reason for leaving were always 'good ones' - i.e. redundancy, or promotion or relocating. In this situation, a standard *reverse chronological* CV will be best for you. It shows you in a good light and your only decision (if, that is, you are looking for career progression in the same field of work) is what kind of profile to add for yourself.

If, however, you have had a chequered career, or you want to diversify, or you are a returner, then clearly this CV will not do you justice. You need one that will highlight your skills, abilities and achievements.

At this stage you will already know yourself whether a standard CV is suitable for you or whether you could prosper from another kind. Either way, it is still worth considering all the options. It could be that now you have spent all this time on it, you would prefer to have more than one style of CV - and I would certainly recommend that to anyone. Especially those who might be interested in pursuing more than one line of work.

Use These Words!

Your prompt list:

achieved	administered	analysed	acquired
acquisitions	arranged	audited	arbitrated
accounted	built	capable	competent
communicated	consistent	controlled	co-ordinated

created	developed	directed	designed
delivered	dealt	economical	efficient
energetic	engineered	established	expanded
experienced	expertise	evaluated	guided
implemented	improved	resourceful	initiated
instructed	led	managed	motivated
negotiated	maintained	organised	participated
positive	processed	productive	produced
provided	planned	promoted	protected
presented	qualified	repaired	sold
successful	supervised	trained	versatile
varied			

Let this list be the starting point for you; find out more and add to it - try the Thesaurus but listen to others - copy these words you hear from now on; add them to all the letters and CVs you write.

8 YOUR ACTION PLAN

● Start with a goal

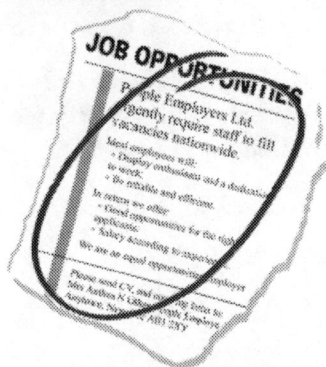

If you have actually been carrying out your own research as you have been reading this book; or at least thinking about your own situation in the light of what you have read so far, you will now be prepared to think about a *plan of action* for yourself.

Every single day each of us prepares a mental plan of action ranging from the simple What shall I do today? What shall I have to eat? to more sophisticated arrangements, such as arranging a wedding, a christening, a holiday. Yet I have never met a client who already had a plan worked out for their career or future work. It seems so simple, so obvious, yet so few of us do it. Why not?

Perhaps the people I meet had a plan, but long-term unemployment disillusioned them, defeated their aspirations; whatever the reason, the simple fact is, you won't get very far without a good plan.

Everything so far mentioned in this book has been a preparation of some kind; looking at external factors that affect your search for work; the job market, places of information, one's own situation. From now on the emphasis will be placed on making choices, making plans based on those choices, and putting that plan into action.

Employment Services spell out the system of action planning with what they call the *Smart* principle. They say that all good plans incorporate the following:

- *S*pecific
- *M*easurable
- *A*chievable
- *R*ealistic
- *T*imebound

If you have not so far looked at all the information that is available, by all means carry on reading but, I stress, *do not make any final decisions until you know everything that is on offer.*

Action planning then.

- *Firstly,* it can cover any period of time.
- *Secondly,* you do not need to have only one.
- *Thirdly,* one master plan will almost certainly be enhanced by several, more precise ones, covering each stage of the larger plan.

Start With A Goal

If you have done the exercises so far mentioned, you will have your skills sheets ready. You will have had several thoughts come to mind as you have been reading, so already you will have some ideas floating around. You might also have dismissed some as being beyond your reach. The SMART plan says you must be realistic in your goals but this can work both ways. More often I see people put themselves down, they think they are not capable of doing what they really want to - when in fact they could. For some reason, wanting something badly makes us enlarge that thing in our minds so that it stretches out of our reach.

Now is not the time to be coy; you can complete this plan alone, you do not have to worry about other people's opinions of what you are striving for. *Be honest with yourself.*

What would you like to be doing in five years time?

- How far away, in terms of skills and experience, are you from that goal now? One thing that completing your own skills sheets should have done is highlight any gaps you might have between your skills and experience now and your ultimate job goal. This will be very useful for your action planning.

- Do you have contacts in your chosen field? - i.e. *networking*

- Did you have the relevant skills, but are rusty, in need of brushing them up?

- Or do you not have the skills, just the yearning to do the job, the conviction that you could do it with the right training?

- Okay, so you don't have a single GCSE, you've always had unskilled jobs, but you never really 'fitted in' with the others, liked the things they liked, or ever seemed to be able to talk to them about anything. You spend your time reading and wished you had stayed on at school. But you don't even know if you're capable of learning. You occasionally see people who have taken courses, and wish... but you wonder if they're much brighter than you...

Well, there's no point in sitting there wondering; you're on the dole and you've got time on your hands - what have you got to lose? If you don't like a course, you can drop out; if you're no good at it, you can drop out; if it is beyond your capability, you can drop out - *you're under no obligation to continue at any time!*

But that's not your action plan completed: that is only a small part of it.

So you are going to sign on for a course at night class. It is free for as long as you are unemployed so there is no problem there; your only decision is what subject to take.

Pick something you'll like, for that is what you'll do best at.

Do that *this week* - whatever else you decide, it won't conflict and, if it does later... you can drop out. Nothing you learn is *ever* wasted. Even if you don't complete the course, you still have the amount you learned. It is like trying to stop smoking; the more times you attempt it, the greater chance of your success in the end.

- So, your Action Plan doesn't need to be specific; it does not have to say *I will get a degree*. It only needs to say; *I will take further education.* For if, at this stage, you have had no further education, you can have no idea how you will take to it.

- *I will upgrade my skills* - that is good enough for now, because by opening the first door, you will merely place yourself in a corridor full of doors and they are all your choices.

You are going to take a course (as they are free, take at least a couple!) You are going to upgrade your skills - how are you going to do that?

- In full-time work
- In a voluntary capacity - if you are very rusty, that might be the best option for the sake of your confidence
- Or in a training scheme?

Perhaps, just thinking along these lines, you have realised that there is actually a course which combines both elements and now you are really working out your action plan. But perhaps not. Perhaps you have always worked in a factory but you were involved in a trade union; you found that the aspect of rules and regulations, the laws surrounding employment, fascinated you and you seemed to have a flair for it (even though your employer might not have been very grateful to you).

You could sign up for English (because you need to brush up on that for any academic subject) and Law at your local night classes. You can also continue searching for work in the areas where you are presently skilled.

So that side of the plan is specific enough for the moment. Turn now to the rest of it.

What are you going to do with the rest of the time?

- Do you want an income above all else?

- Do you want to be back in full-time, paid employment?

- Okay, so you have your skills sheet, you know whether you want to return to the same kind of work as before or not - you know whether you can or not (i.e. if that kind of work is available).

So how are you going to reach that goal?

- Are you prepared, as we went into earlier in the *preparation* section? If not, then you need to go back to that and make your preparations accordingly.

So now, your Action Plan should look like this:

Short, medium and long term: Upgrade Skills

- *How?* By taking FE courses.

- *What in?* Law and English.

- *How long for?* GCSE = one year.

- *Afterwards?* Unknown.

So far, that fulfils all the criteria of a *Smart* plan; it is specific, achievable, measurable and it is realistic. Of course, it is timebound; you will start as soon as possible and the course will last for one year, attending classes two nights a week (one night for each class).

Medium and long term: Find Work

- *How?* All methods available.
- *What kind?* List three options here.
- *Who can help me?* Employment Services, own enquiries.
- *How long for?* Maximum of six months.
- *Afterwards?* Unknown; perhaps continue upgrading skills; perhaps promotion; perhaps diversification.

Short term: Find Help and Information for all of Above

- *How?* Ask for help and advice.
- *Where?* Job Centre, Library, Careers Information Service, Colleges.
- *How long for?* Now, set yourself a limit here or you might waste time wavering in indecision - *two weeks* to decide on courses and enrol!

Now then, this plan of action is *Smart* in all aspects but it has one more quality, and that is it is *flexible*.

You could find that education is where you really find your talent, in which case you can switch to concentrating all your energies on that. You can find the opposite and, again, switch. You could find that your evening classes go on and on, so in three years time, you have your A levels and then start looking to Universities for a degree course. Your confidence level has shot up because you found a job. It increased further because of your courses. You now have skills in studying techniques and you will be a very attractive proposition to a University: they like mature students!

By the same token, attending evening classes and one or more of the government sponsored job-search courses, you almost certainly increase your job prospects. One of the reasons why it is harder for an unemployed person to find work than it is for someone in work, is that they cannot show an employer what they have been doing. After a long spell of being out of work poverty and disillusionment show in every aspect of that person; their demeanour, their body language. Attending these courses will liven you up no end! You will have something to talk about. Research has shown that an interviewer looks for enthusiasm and you will have that again - at last.

If you decide to take your education even further after the first year, your employer will respect you and, if it is a large company, you could well find yourself with an offer of promoted employment for when you complete your degree. But, of course, you still don't even have an O-level, do you? You're jumping ahead...*but don't abandon these ideas: Keep them open: They are realistic: They are measurable!* You can't measure your ability to obtain a BA before you have even obtained a GCSE but, like everything else, you must take one step at a time. Don't slam the door before you've even looked through it.

But that isn't the end of your Action Planning.

Your choices do not have to lie at either the 'straight into work' or 'Further Education' poles but at somewhere in between - or even dotted all the way along the line.

Are your skills rusty?

If they are, then a retraining or refresher course could be the answer for you. If these were purely physical skills then there are many courses open to you, just as there are if they were professional ones. Again, your Job Centre is the place to start to enquire about this but if you opt for one of their 'Back to Work' courses then you will almost certainly be informed of all your options there.

Would you like to develop new skills?

Again, you would enquire about these at Job Centre or on one of their courses. Job Plan, for instance, arranges for visiting speakers on their one week course. These come from TEC and LEC or from Community Action. They tell you what they can offer and if you are interested then you can have a chat with them afterwards. You can visit their premises if you like, see what it's like, if you would enjoy it. They can train you in such a diverse range of skills from secretarial to signwriting, from care work to mechanics.

So your action plan could have three elements here; the further education courses, your job search which you could do at Job Club, and perhaps a retraining course. One good thing is that there is no cutting of options by taking the Employment Services courses. If you take, say Job Plan, you can take Job Plan immediately after or you could take one of the retraining schemes and then take Job Plan, and so on. None of these will increase your bank account but they will certainly make you feel as though you are coming alive again! And, if you involve yourself in retraining and further education, you are also probably increasing your ultimate earning power.

How does your Action Plan look now?

- *Short term*: Check out *all options* by visiting Job Centre for an interview with a claimants advisor. Visit library, careers information, colleges.

- *Sign up for relevant courses*. Make sure they don't clash.

- Job Plan or Job Search Seminar are short courses and so they will easily fit into the short term category.

- *Medium term*: Retraining Scheme or Training for Work or Community Action or Job Club.

- Also you will start your further education courses which will continue for a year.

- *Long term*: Security of salary, of employment, increase of prospects (you thought you 'just wanted a job', did you?). By now your skills should have increased nicely, you probably have at least a couple of GCSEs and might be considering an HND or other qualification. If you are in work you could consider applying for one of their courses which you can study on day release from work or, if you have really become hooked on further education (as tends to happen with mature students) you could now be considering the Open Learning or Open University courses. They are not as expensive as you might think (if you're in work) and of course, they have concessions for the unemployed.

During this time, new doors will be opening as you develop your skills, increase your confidence, and you will be able to carry out frequent reassessments of yourself. At any point from here on you could find yourself back in work and so that, too, will require several shifts of plan *but by no means abandon your Action Plan*: you can still develop and follow it.

How are your interpersonal skills?

If you have been out of work for a long time you could have become isolated, and being back working with a lot of people can come as quite a culture shock. You can brush up on these skills too, if you have a mind to. This would mean *adding to your Action Plan.*

Self development in itself can become addictive. It might seem impossible now, as you contemplate your first ever action plan. As you move on through it, watching one plan after another being accomplished and get to the point where you can look back and see just how far you have travelled in terms of skill, confidence, knowledge and personal control, this in itself can spur you on to develop further.

One final suggestion: don't forget to add to your action plan any small items you want to develop; if your writing skills aren't all they need to be to apply for jobs, write that in. So too, with interview techniques - anything that is a factor at all should be added, no matter how small or insignificant it might seem.

9 YOU'LL NEED A REFERENCE

- Volunteering can pay off
- Who should give you a reference?

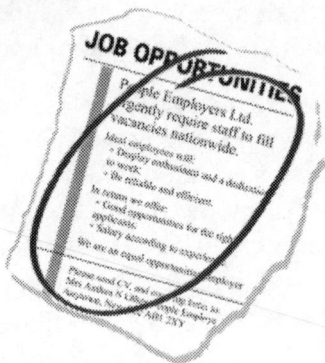

You might think it is odd to have the chapter on references so early in the book - surely it is the last thing that you need in your search for work, coming after a successful interview?

You need to be prepared long before you reach the interview stage, and once you start to apply for jobs, you can have no idea when someone is going to ask you for your referees. Therefore, it is necessary to sort that out now. If you are going to list the names and addresses of your referees on your CV, then you need to contact those people now, to obtain their permission and to forewarn them that from here on they might be receiving enquiries about you.

References are very important today. The more recent they are, the better your prospects, but my contention is that nothing is insurmountable if you focus on a problem. If you can categorise it, the answer is usually easy.

The worst then; you have no reference at all. Either you have never had a job or you left under a cloud; one can be as bad as the other. Fact number one: *you have to get a reference.*

Volunteering Can Pay Off

Your references don't have to be from employers. You can look for a character reference - usually from someone in a respectable field. If you do voluntary work, you are in the perfect place. Ask the organiser if he will give you a reference.

If you have no one at all you can turn to then take something like *community action*. This is where you work in a voluntary capacity. The list of places is endless, and you can go into virtually any field you like.

The benefits:

- you will learn new skills,
- make new friends,
- prove yourself to be reliable,
- hardworking,
- dedicated,
- full of initiative.

All the things you need for a reference.

If you organise it through your local Job Centre, then you can continue with your search for work and you will be confident that you will have recent references when you need them.

Old references

If you haven't worked for a few years, again you could have a problem. Perhaps you have lost touch with your employer, the business has moved, gone into liquidation, or the job was temporary and unlikely to prove favourable simply through lack of memory. I would strongly recommend some kind of voluntary work. Just the proof that you are a good time-keeper, of pleasant personality, reliable, will be enough to impress any employer if you have already provided an excellent letter and a good interview. The problem is, without any kind of reference, you leave too many question marks.

But don't take any kind of voluntary work just to obtain references. Look at what is on offer. If you can't find something that specifically relates to your chosen field of work, then look to your hobbies.

Ask yourself throughout, if the voluntary work will enhance your CV. I have encountered many examples when it was so misplaced that it created difficulties; if you want to become a carer, for instance, then working in a local charity shop is not really relevant. If, however, you have a long involvement with that particular charity then it *does* become relevant.

Also, you're not being paid for this work, so choose something that matters to you - perhaps something you would not normally be able to do. In the North Staffs area, a charitable wildlife centre is crying out for dedicated people to go in and help with the wildlife. This is not 'dogsbody' work but real 'hands on' experience with wild, injured animals - have you any idea how qualified one must normally be in order to get into that kind of work? To me, loving animals, this seems like a 'once in a lifetime' opportunity; one from which I am now barred by definition of being *in* work. If you have the chance in your area, jump at it!

Many people simply don't know about these things. They are caught up in their problems of unemployment, fear of not being able to get back into work, they walk into the Job Centre, look at the vacancies and don't know about the rest. If you ask for a personal interview, they will tell you about everything that is on offer. You won't have to make a decision there and then, but go away, think about it, perhaps go back and ask further questions. You won't be considered to be a time-waster; you will get onto first name terms with your Job Centre and that can be very profitable to you.

That is if you have no references at all; but what if you simply don't know who to contact?

Who Should Give You A Reference?

Usually, you need two referees. At least one of these should be a past or present employer. If you know that your most recent employer will give a good reference, then you have no problem. For the second reference choose between another ex-employer or a good character referee. For this, it is always best to choose someone of 'public standing'; that is, a Justice of the Peace, a doctor, a Headmaster. Of course, if you can secure the reference of someone in a senior position in the field you are trying to enter, that is even better - whether you have worked for them or not. A company really wants to have a second opinion once they have made up their own minds about you, so simply go for the best you can get.

10 WRITING A CV

- Length
- Format
- Prompt lists
- Styles of CV
- So what do CVs look like?

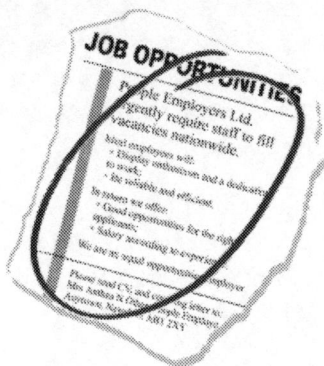

It seems that, whatever your employment aspirations, a CV is now essential. And it is an expensive item. A friend told me he had been quoted seventy-five pounds for one - a stock-broker, you'd think? A company director demanding gilt-edged paper? He is a farm labourer and this was the price he had been quoted from a company which advertised in a farming magazine. I simply advise this: if you do not already have a CV then write, phone or visit your local Job Centre right now and apply to go on one of the courses run by Employment Services which provides CVs.

Perhaps you already have one, have been using it for years, still have plenty of copies left? Firstly, if you have had it for a while, it is probably out of date in terms of your job skills and experience but there is a stronger reason why it should be updated. Nothing seems to date as quickly as a CV and the style will show just how long you have been out of work.

Length

It used to be that the longer the CV the more impressive it was. A five page CV tells of a person with a long, distinguished career history. Not any more; it tells of long-windedness, lack of awareness of the current moves in the employment field.

When I had my last CV drawn up, the rule was for two pages, then it changed to one page. Now it tends to be moving back to two-pages - but with a different format.

Format

There is now the option of 'Profiles' whereby you use just two or three sentences to 'sum up your character'. These are good - if you can get them right - but do not rush one. Spend time - a lot of time - and preferably seek opinion on them.

In a decade where *'Time is money'* is a common saying and, perhaps more importantly, where any given vacancy might have over two hundred applicants, a long, rambling CV will not be appreciated. It is a way of getting yourself binned. And therefore defeating your objective.

The following is a rundown of all the information about yourself that you will need at hand in order to compile your CV. You won't necessarily use all of the information for that will depend on what type of CV you choose for yourself; but you do need it ready just in case. If you completed the previous *skills* exercises, you should already be well prepared for all this.

- Personal Details

  If you put your age (and my advice is *do not*) then put date of birth, not age in years. Otherwise your CV will be out of date by your next birthday.

- Education

  If you list examinations then say also what grades you achieved, but if you are a graduate then you no longer have to list every part of the degree you studied: BA; the subject; the grade, will suffice.

- Training

  If you have taken any of the many training courses on offer, you place the details here.

- Career History

  It used to be that you listed every job you had ever had; then that moved to listing the last ten years. Now, the current feeling is to list only the last two jobs you have had.

- Hobbies and Interests

  You can list what you do in your spare time but remember that the interviewer will almost certainly bring the subject up (usually to help put you at your ease) - so don't list something just because you think it sounds good, when in fact you know nothing about it.

- Additional Information

  This is to add anything you think might help with your application. A driving licence, of course, would go here, but also anything more specific to the job in question.

- References

  People do not seem to be putting the names and addresses of referees on their CVs these days. 'Available upon request' is becoming more and more frequent, and doesn't really need stating; either include the names and addresses, or don't. You must still have your referees though; and be able to forward their details promptly if the employer asks for them.

- Brevity

  The key phrase here is; *be precise*. Don't use any word that is wasting the space. Don't say;' I used to be a leader at the local Boy Scouts Club' when you can say 'Scout Leader'. You have one sheet of A4 paper; there are only seventy-four lines on it; you can only fit about ten words to a line. You have to leave decent margins and tidy paragraphs and clear spacing; so in the space that is left, make every word count.

Having said that...

It is your CV. It is to show you, give a picture of you, your 'calling card', if you like.

If you listen to the current thoughts on CVs and decide you don't like what you hear, then consider it, weigh up the pros and cons - and if you still feel the same, *stick to your own method.*

Now that you have all these headings, you need to allocate space to them according to what you think is important in the light of the kind of work you are looking for. Is experience more important than qualifications - or the other way around?

In the pub trade, for instance, experience is very important so if you worked as a barmaid in half a dozen different establishments while your children were small, you want them all included. Especially if they were owned by the same brewery. You would have difficulty finding space for all this on a one-page CV, but could include a second page of specific experience. Alternatively, instead of listing all the jobs, you could simply say you have 'X number of years' in the field. Don't forget, also, that the company might forward their own standard application form for this.

Prompt Lists

This is for those of you who might only be reading this section on CVs and therefore skipped the skills exercises. If you did complete them then you do not need to go through these paragraphs, so move on to *styles of* CV. This is important because it is the planning which goes into the making of a CV which is so difficult and time-consuming. You must have all the correct dates for schooling, exams, training and work history - and if you are in your thirties this is no *easy* task!

Dates

Some people seem to have amazing memories for dates.

People in their fifties who remember the exact date of leaving school; every exam they sat; every date they started and left jobs. This is by no means the norm; most are like me - they groan when someone asks them the date, and their brains go blank when they are asked, 'Just give me the year, then.' For such people, there is no option but to sit down with a sheet of paper and 'backtrack' over their lives. 'Well, I was eleven when I went to secondary school; born 1957 + 11 = *Ah!* 1968. Now, when did I leave? I was fifteen; 1968 + 4 = Oh yes, 1972 - *American Pie!*... Now, what was that first job...' Moreover, if your career history is 'bitty' - fragmented - and you did as I did in the seventies, flitting from one job to another, you will have some 'honest doctoring' to do before it can look neat on a CV. You want to retain all the experience you gained but lose all the space-consuming details.

A good prompt list and skills sheets are invaluable for this and you will amaze yourself at how much you have achieved; that in itself will make you feel more confident.

The important thing is, for each 'experience' you list - whether that is education or work or hobby - list dates and addresses. If it was a course, then list exams (and dates) subjects and grades.

You almost certainly won't use all this information on your CV but you need it laid out clearly in front of you in order to choose what to include and what to discard.

Styles Of CV

The ordinary CV is the *reverse chronological CV*. That is, it begins today, and works backward in time. This is very useful when;

- The last employer is highly credible - a well-known, respected organisation.

- The next career move is in the same field (and it is 'upwardly mobile').

- The career history shows a natural growth and development.

With the reverse chronological CV, it tends to start with personal details, work through education and career and end with 'additional information'.

But this kind of CV is not useful when;

- Your work record is intermittent.
- You are seeking change.
- Changes of employment are frequent.
- When there might be some other reason for you to think you might be seen at a disadvantage; age, lack of direct skills, women returning to work after child-rearing.
- Redundancy from a place where you have worked for many years.

Profiles

For the categories which reverse chronological CVs do not help, the *profile* is much more useful. It lists all the same details but in the reverse order, putting the emphasis on skills and experience rather than the more traditional things such as age, qualifications, then specific job history.

This places emphasis on your skills and strengths and allows you to organise and present them in a much more positive way. It puts you firmly in control of the information you are putting forward and allows much more flexibility in the information you want to get across.

Résumés

In the first edition of this book, I claimed that none of these types of CV was better than the other. However, I began to monitor the use of résumés and I found that they are hugely successful. So much so that I began to warn everyone to use them. Where clients were sceptical, I suggested they write both a traditional CV and a résumé, and give the résumé a trial run first. Not one of these clients ever returned to using the traditional CV.

People who had not secured a single interview with the 'reverse chronological' CV suddenly had success with their résumé. Moreover, many clients reported that interviewers had specifically asked where they had obtained their CV and said they had appreciated the lack of 'waffle' and irrelevant detail. This is the point of the résumé - *say what you can do for the employer and leave the rest out.*

The other single factor which was seen to make great impact on interviews, was the Personal Profile and this I would now recommend as essential to any CV.

However, it is for you to decide which would work best for you. If you have your own word processor, or access to one, that is ideal for there is nothing but time to stop you from trying several out.

There is another aspect which can alter any of these CVs, and that is whether you are targeting a specific company or field of work. If you do only want one kind of employment then why waste time and words by making out a general CV? You might as well go for it and state it clearly on the page. If you want to teach in further education then say, immediately below your name and address:

Job Target: Teacher of Further Education

Knowing what you want and being determined to go out and get it will not work against you with any employer - although the reverse might.

The hard work begins...

If you thought that the exercises were difficult, listing all those wonderful skills you didn't know you had and searching through your memory for all those dates, places and reasons; just be glad you did it earlier. This stage is time-consuming enough as it is without the added burden of all that to go through again.

This is also the final (uphill) struggle and the part where you will achieve the real pay-off. You will have created your own CV which will never be so hard again but will only ever need occasional updating.

The first thing then; *what constitutes a bad CV?*

- It is scruffy, untidy, badly laid out.
- It is on poor quality paper.
- Mistakes - spelling, grammar, typing errors.
- Badly photocopied.
- It is too long.
- The information is badly organised, making it difficult to read.
- The CV doesn't seem to bear any relevance to the job vacancy.
- Loose writing - long rambling sentences.
- Too Spartan - essential facts are listed only, giving no idea of the personality of the sender.

Have you defined your target?

If you have, you have made life much easier for yourself because you will already know what information to leave out as being irrelevant. Or, at least, you will see it clearly as you progress through your own CV. Even if you can't be as specific as saying, 'I want to teach English in a college of further education.' you could perhaps short-list your options down to two or three types of work.

If you haven't done this, I would suggest you spend some time now going back over your skills sheets and try to come up with some final decisions in this area. Even if you can't decide finally between two very different career paths. 'I would like to teach *but*, if I can't get into that I'd like to go back to retail management.' Then at least you will know that you need to make two very different CVs - because you can't mix and match something as diverse as that! Better to focus on each career individually, and then target each with their own CV. But if you are still wavering at this stage, I promise you, *it will show up on your CV*. It will make you look indecisive. Even if you are indecisive, you don't need to be obvious about it!

So What Do CVs Look Like?

The standard format for a reverse chronological one page CV:

CURRICULUM VITAE
Personal Details Name: Date of Birth: Address: Marital Status: General Health: Telephone No:
Education
Training
Work History
Spare Time Activities
Additional Information
References

Fig. 1. The standard format for a reverse chronological one page CV
(ES Crown Copyright 1995)

Standard format adapted to a particular person:

CURRICULUM VITAE

Personal Details

Name:	Lisa Alison Cooper
Address:	908 Plymouth Grove,
	Allerton, Leicester,
	AL2 5BJ
Telephone No:	(0776) 501292

Education

1990 - 1995   Kingsway Secondary School for girls

Qualifications

CSEs English (1), Art (2), Needlework (2), Domestic Science (2),
RSA I Typing (Credit)

Achievements

Regularly number 1 in the class for English Language.
Often chosen to deliver literary passages for my year at 'Parents Days'.
Selected every year for school netball team.
Won first prize in school art competition (1983).

Additional Information

Much of my time spent helping old people in my local area, shopping,
washing and cleaning. Also enjoy babysitting for friends and relations.
I communicate well, in both spoken and written forms, and presently attend
night school studying RSA II and English Literature.

Leisure Interests

Reading, keep fit, cinema.

References

Ms J. Pearson	Mr A. Fletcher
Headmistress	12 Bankside Gardens
Kingsway Secondary School for Girls	Dorwen
Heathland Road	AL4 2BJ
Allerton	
Leicester	
AL2 6SQ	

Fig.2. (ES Crown Copyright 1995)

Comment: You can see clearly from this that Lisa Cooper is a recent school leaver because no 'career history' has been included. However, she has presented herself in a positive light by listing her achievements and stating clearly that she has not been wasting her time but is continuing her studies at night classes. Her referee is impressive and reassuring as it is her headmistress.

Reverse chronological one page CV - with chronological work history

(*see Fig. 3*) *Comment:* I assume, because of the alteration in dates from reverse chronology to starting with his first job, that Resham's foray into self-employment didn't work out and he is now seeking factory work again. If that is so then he has done the right thing by reversing his career history (the rule is to start with your present or last job and work backwards). His repeated mention of his family (under Marital Status and Spare Time Activities) show him to be a keen family man, a stable background (look at his interests) and no real interests outside of work and home. This is a good CV for that kind of target; an employer is looking for someone who will learn, will fit in, and this applicant shows all the right signs.

Reverse chronological one page CV - with a specific target

(*see Fig. 4.*) *Comment:* This is an excellent example of where reverse chronology works - and the positive use of specific targeting. This person clearly intends to make a career of retail management and with the current lucrative and attractive packages, why not!

I would, however, question why this person is not already a manager; has he been bypassed for some reason?

CURRICULUM VITAE

Personal Details

Name: Mr Resham Singh Johal   **Date of Birth**: 2.7.48
Marital Status: Married,
Address: 12 Russell Close, have two children
Nottingham.
Telephone No: (01776) 501292   **General Health**: Good

Education
Received General Education in India.

Work History
1979 - 1984   Beeston Boiler Foundry, Beeston, Nottingham. Boiler
Grinder.
General duties entailed the grinding of boilers: a fairly
responsible job which had to be checked for leaks, if
unsatisfactory then had to be put right. Had to operate a
grinding machine to do the job.
1986 - July '87 Hicking Pentecost, London Rd, Nottingham. Machine Operator.
Duties entailed the changing of rollers on a pressing
machine.
Jan '88 - Dec '89 Self-employed. Ran a Fish and Chip shop in Nottingham.
General duties included the day-to-day running of the
shop, serving customers, handling cash, operating a till,
paying wages etc.

Spare Time Activities
Where time allows, I like to watch television and video, listen to music,
watch various types of sports, especially cricket. I also enjoy spending time
with my wife and children.

Additional Information
I am a keen, conscientious, hard-working and reliable person. I am a very
good time-keeper and enjoy meeting people, and can adapt to any
environment. I would like to use my skills to make a positive contribution to
my place of work and get on well individually and also as a member of a
team.

References
Available upon request.

Fig.3. (ES Crown Copyright 1995)

CURRICULUM VITAE

Winston John Napper

21 St. Annes Road, East Dulwich, London, ED1 2JP

Telephone No: 0130 655845

Retail Sales Assistant

With extensive experience in the audio, video and domestic appliance field

CAREER HISTORY

HITEX-LTD - January 84 to November 87 - Selling specialist Hifi's, plus conventional home entertaining equipment, particularly TVs, personal computers, photographic equipment. Won 'Employee of the Month Award' 3 times for: Highest Sales Achievement, 'Best Trainee' (on Company Product Training Course) and for my design of 2 new customer record systems which saved the branch £240 per year.

MURRAMS ELECTRICAL - August 81 to January 84 - Selling a wide range of Hifi, Television and Domestic Appliances. Control of store and 3 staff in Manager's absence.

T. HALL & SONS (Meat & Handy Foods) - September 80 to August 81 - Casual production assistant.

Education:	Broadway Secondary School - Sept. 75 to July 80
Qualifications:	CSEs in Maths (1), Chemistry (1), English (1), Computer Science (2), Geography (4)
Leisure Interests:	Football, Snooker, Computing, Music
Additional Information:	Captain of local football team (presently 3rd in County League Division 2). Clean driving licence. Ready to start immediately
Personal Details:	Date of birth: 10.8.64 Marital Status: Single Health: Excellent
References:	Minimum of 3, AVAILABLE ON REQUEST

Fig.4. (ES Crown Copyright 1995)

Perhaps, if I were in that profession I would know about the previous companies he has worked for. Some retail companies only recruit graduates for their management positions and it could be that Winston is moving on to a company where prospects would be better for his background of hands-on experience. I would have advised him to replace his 'Job Target' at the top of the page with 'Retail Management'. I would also like to see this CV laid out in a profile or résumé format, using his skills sheet to present a more vigorous, assertive approach. He is unemployed at the moment ('ready to start immediately') but look how little emphasis is placed on that and how positively he shows himself.

Profile CVs

(see Fig. 5) *Comment:* This CV was kindly given to me by someone who had accepted voluntary redundancy from their company. The company in question actually paid for these CVs to be compiled for their employees and they clearly brought in a good agency to deal with it.

It is an excellent example of how present-day negative factors in job seeking can be overcome.

Firstly, on the surface, it might seem that this person is unskilled for any other type of work as he has only really had one job since he left school - and in a fairly specialised area at that.

Secondly, this is a case where the reverse chronological CV would have done no favours for the job seeker - he is over fifty and left school without qualifying (in the days when one did so).

Another factor which isn't directly stated, but which an employer would notice, is that the applicant enjoys a cultured and fairly middle-class lifestyle (the address, which has been altered, confirms this). One positive conclusion an employer would come to is that any factory worker who enjoys these benefits is a good worker - and wants overtime!

His age, which is often assumed to work against someone in this situation, is slotted in neatly on the second page - endorsing that it is of no relevance - whilst all the important details are stated boldly on page one.

CURRICULUM VITAE

PAUL SMITH

ADDRESS: 1 Anywhere Street
                     Burton-on-Trent
                     Staffordshire
                     DE1 ABC

TELEPHONE NO: 01283 123456

PROFILE:
A conscientious and reliable hardworking employee with extensive experience in manufacturing. A quick learner. Quality conscious, having worked within a BS 5750 environment. Excellent attendance and time-keeping record. Can work in a team or on own initiative. Used to working to deadlines and under pressure.

Fig.5, continued overleaf (ES Crown Copyright 1995)

KEY SKILLS AND EXPERIENCE:
Various production machine skills
Adaptable and flexible
Experienced in working in Kan Ban, J.I.T. and T.P.M. Systems
Good Basic Mechanical and D.I.Y. Skills

CAREER HISTORY:	**DATES**	
	FROM	**TO**
PIRELLI LTD, BURTON-ON-TRENT	Mar 1960	Aug 1994
Truck Tyre Builder		
Also experienced in other production areas		
BLACKSHAWS GARAGE, BURTON-ON-TRENT	Jan 1960	Mar 1960
Apprentice		

TRAINING, EDUCATION AND QUALIFICATIONS:
1955 - 1957   Woodville C.S.E.
1957 - 1959   Granville C.S.E.
Good Standard of Education

PERSONAL DETAILS:
Married with 2 Children aged 26 and 29
House Owner
Full Clean Driving Licence
Non-smoker
Excellent Health
Date of Birth: 20.10.44

INTERESTS:
D.I.Y.
Reading
Rambling
Gardening
Car Maintenance
Winemaking
Assisting Burton Carers by Fundraising etc

Fig.5 (ES Crown Copyright 1995)

The Functional Résumé

This is my favourite CV (*see Fig. 6*). I met this man when he came to give a talk about what he could offer in the areas of Training For Work or Community Action. I, and everyone else in the room, was enthralled. He was impressive and you trusted his word. Not because he boasted but because he showed his record, he offered his credentials and then he went on to say what he had come to say.

He mentioned CVs, said he had brought his own for anyone to inspect and so at the end of his talk, I asked if I could look at it.

This man gives no personal information at all; other than his name, he does not even refer to gender; there is no age, no referees, no educational background, and no specific job history is given. When I explained what I wanted the CV for, he said, 'Yes, sure, if you want to use it' and then he laughed and said, rather cryptically, 'It definitely works...'

Just look at the wealth of forceful, positive words he has used. Just glancing down the page there is; motivated, management experience, career, positive, pragmatic, proven record, activities, success, innovative, ability, achiever - *that is just in the first two sentences!* He doesn't reduce the force with what follows either but continues his advancement on the senses: negotiator, responsibility, development, control, responsibility *again*. This word continues to appear throughout as does negotiator and control. Another repeated word is 'promoted'.

After five minutes in this man's company, you just don't doubt a word he says. His CV doesn't mention his ability to motivate others or to inspire confidence in people but that is just what I saw him do.

Kenneth Cyril Taylor
Chapel House
44 Upper Way
Upper Longdon
Nr Rugeley
Telephone: (0543) 490532   Staffs WS15 2QD

PERSONAL PROFILE

A highly motivated manager with extensive sales and management experience in the oil industry having been employed by Shell Oil for most of his career covering a wide range of sales activities in differing market sectors. A positive and pragmatic team player with a proven record of success; innovative, with an ability to make things happen and an achiever.

KEY SKILLS

Maximising sales potential.

Self motivated.

Proven Contract negotiation ability.

Market knowledge.

Ability to instill confidence and brand loyalty.

CAREER WITH SHELL UK OIL COMPANY

1982 - 1994 Burgess Fuels Limited - Shell Distributor

Appointment as Retail Sales Negotiator for the total delivery area covered by Burgess Fuels Limited in the West Midlands area with responsibility for the development and retention of Dealer owned retail outlets in the 1.5 - 2 M/Ltr throughput range. Having complete control and responsibility for every aspect of site operation.

With regard to existing outlets this consisted of all aspects of Contract negotiation and resigning, site signalisation, product deliveries and credit management, incorporating control and administration of price support activities, co-ordination of customer account and installation of electronic system for credit card activites relating to sales.

Competitor acquisitions were an important element and were aggressively pursued with success in this area being evident in a 37% increase in throughput.

Fig.6. Functional Résumé

11 INITIAL APPROACHES

- Use psychology
- Stick to the point

You have taken stock, you have looked at the job market, you have made some choices and have a plan of action. You have also decided upon and contacted referees; they know to expect calls over the next few weeks. You have your CVs ready to send out and all the other resources necessary to start your job-search. With so much good preparation behind you, you must be raring to go.

What method are you going to use to contact prospective employers?

If you are determined to succeed, then you will use every method at your disposal and you won't abandon any unless you have proved yourself both incapable of using that method - and incapable of improving it.

The methods to use are:

- Speculative letters
- Speculative phonecalls
- Speculative visits
- Standard application forms
- Following up advertised vacancies
- Daily visits to the job centre

and also:

- Constant networking

The skills and techniques for these all differ and are perhaps also affected by mood.

Use Psychology

If you are despondent, in a depressed mood or suffering from low self-esteem today, the first way in which it will show is through your voice. You will sound dull, too quiet, your voice won't be so distinct. I would not recommend that you make phone calls that day; but I would certainly suggest that you send out at least a dozen of that speculative letter that you have already prepared for yourself.

If you wake up in a particularly good mood, full of life, energy, the sun is shining; that is the day for speculative visits. Put your best clothes on and take yourself off round the businesses you are targeting. It is surprising how much success you can generate in this way.

Efficiency, of course, is best used in the office. If this is the way you feel then the phone, the word-processor and the photocopier will show best results.

Whatever your mood, whatever clothes you are wearing, wherever you are, you can always carry out networking. Treat every business like a prospective employer; even the local shopping trip. Try out your style, your technique, ask about how business is doing, strike up conversations. You will get feedback, even if only in terms of friendliness, which in turn will make you feel good, increase your confidence.

Use all the methods at your disposal; but use them in a way which is right for you. Know yourself and listen to your own inner voice. Ask for advice, listen to it, but don't be afraid to reject it if you are sure it is not right for you. There is much advice which I offer people which I do not use myself; because I know that it is not my style, or would give too false an impression of myself to a possible employer. I offer information which I know is right for someone; which I have seen work for others, or myself.

One thing that I have seen however, and which I know works, and that is: the more business-like your approach to finding work, the more successful and the more quickly you are successful.

Stick To The Point

Always bear in mind what is behind all your actions; you are selling, and not simply yourself, but your labour. The employer is dictating the terms - he is the employer. We have to look at our labour as a commodity that someone is going to buy. It doesn't matter whether we write, phone or visit, we are still selling ourselves and, as any salesman will tell you, you must believe in the product.

Therefore, you must know the product well, its good points, and be able to identify them and communicate them to their best advantage. If you have already completed an action plan for yourself, you should be able to think of several factors immediately. From now on, whenever you look at an advertised vacancy, you should be comparing your skills with those being asked for.

The rest of this book will be concerned with you actively seeking work; that is, putting all the previous chapters into practice. What follows, then, is a concentrated look at the different types of letter you might need in your search for work. I make no apology for the length of this chapter; as with CVs, I believe it is essential to get this section right for it might be the first glimpse that a potential employer has of you. This is the first of the bins that you have to avoid. Get used to that visual image of the giant waste paper bin of which a good ninety per-cent of all applications must fall into; ensure that yours is not one of them.

12 LETTER WRITING

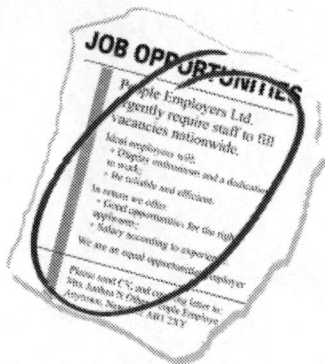

- Some letters examined

As with every approach you make to a prospective employer, the golden rule is: *be brief.*

There are two types of letter you will most commonly use for your job search. One is a formal letter of application which usually covers a CV or application form. The other is a speculative letter which you would also enclose with a CV. In your covering letter brevity is particularly important. Yet at the same time, it is possible to be brief to the point of bad manners. If you simply write;

Sir,
Please find enclosed CV.

Yours sincerely,

Well, you wouldn't would you? *Would you?*

I feel as though I've seen everything in letters and personnel officers must see a whole lot more. Get used to visualising that giant waste paper bin. Get used to envisaging what goes in and what stays on the desk. The example on the previous page is definite 'bin fodder'.

If a sentence consists of 'Subject, Verb, Object' then a letter consists of 'Beginning, Middle, End'.

Try to make three paragraphs. The first is your introduction:

- Tell them why you are writing.
- Be specific; if it is a job vacancy, give the title, the reference number if there was one and where and when you saw the advertisement.

The second paragraph states the point of your contact with them:

- Why you are applying for the job.
- Why you think you should be considered.
- Anything which would enhance your prospects.

The third paragraph invites them to answer back:

- When you would be available for interview.
- If you are available for immediate start, and so on.

  These are the basic rules of meeting people and you can do no better than to show in your covering letter that you are polite, well mannered, and pleasant to know.

If you feel that your CV doesn't say enough about you for this specific job:

- Enlarge upon the necessary areas in the letter.

- But keep to the point.

- Keep the reader interested.

- Don't waste their time with small talk.

- Remember that he or she might have a couple of hundred of these letters to read.

If you are not a good letter writer - and there's nothing lost by recognising this fact - then work on some standard letters that you can adapt to different employers. This is not to say photocopy a letter and send it out *en masse* to specific vacancies.

If an employer senses that you have done this, he will almost certainly lose interest. There is a set format which you can use - a standard introduction and a standard closing statement. But make sure that it is clear you are applying for their vacancy within their company.

There are specific rules concerning the format of letters and we shall look at those in a moment but first a warning about 'the picture' of a letter.

The first thing the person sees when they receive your letter is the envelope; the second thing they see is a piece of paper. I know that this might seem so basic as to defy reference in a book but I have seen letters of application prepared and ready to post that are simply so badly presented that they will ensure that the sender will *not* get the job.

This does not seem to be a symptom of lack of education or training either; it seems to be a simple lack of thought. Perhaps a lack of awareness that there are rules which govern layout and also a psychological factor of what looks good on the page.

So, the simple rules are;

- Make sure that your address is placed neatly, legibly, on the envelope.

- *Best handwriting!* If it isn't - if you have made a mistake - *do it again.* Better to bin your own envelope than have a personnel officer do it for you.

- Make sure that the overall picture of your letter is pleasing. The reader will not zoom in and read a single word until he or she has looked at the page as a whole.

- Make sure that the content of the letter is centred on the page - that is, that it has margins top, bottom, left and right. To be really technical, the margin at the left should be just slightly less than the right; and just slightly more room at the bottom than at the top.

- The next rule is that whereas a CV should be typed, a letter should be handwritten.

- A letter should be written on unlined paper and then, just to make life more difficult, you should ensure that your lines of writing are completely straight. If they slant... there's that bin again.

If your handwriting is wonderful, you are streets ahead in the race to the interview. But if it is untidy, a scrawl? If it looks, as my teacher said to me, like a spider has crawled out of an inkwell and slithered across your paper? Then you have to make a decision as to whether to break the rule, risk your best, or some less honest response. My advice would be never to let someone else to write the letter for you - for that seems, to me, to be dishonest.

I type my letters. I know that my handwriting is never pleasing to the eye and when I am nervous, or writing to a stranger, it is even worse. I am fairly sure that any letter I write by hand will be binned. Therefore, I take my chances with the type-written letter.

There is also another factor to consider these days which is that when a personnel officer has so many letters to contend with, does he or she want to struggle with someone's handwriting? I find that no matter how neatly a person writes, I still have to work harder to understand their handwriting than I would a typewritten letter. I know that the older, the busier, I get, the less patient I am with these things.

But please beware; I am speaking my own personal opinion here, based on my own appalling handwriting - I am not repeating what personnel officers have told me. I would certainly point out that if the prospective employer is a man or woman of 'the old school' they might not only be unimpressed with a typewritten letter, but might be positively offended. You must take your chance with this, based on your own assessment of your own writing.

And I would say, finally, that nothing is more pleasing to the eye and more helpful with one's own handwriting than a traditional fountain pen.

Some Letters Examined

The following examples are all written by the same person, in the same batch. That is, the person gathered together a list of immediate vacancies from that day's advertisements and responded in the following way. Though they are not perfect and can be criticised, they all delivered the desired results; ie the invitation to interview for the job.

Request for application form

The first one, then, is a simple request for an application form (*see Fig. 7*). This could be seen as the simplest of the lot but note that the writer has ensured that, although brief, the letter does not appear terse. Also, this can be the most difficult letter to type because of getting the layout right. In this, the writing has been well-centred and is neat.

Letters to breweries

In this letter, (*see Fig. 8*) the writer is aware that there is a specific system used by each company and that too much information will be wasted because all breweries use their own standard application forms. However, breweries will rarely look at an applicant without knowing that they have some relevant experience.

The writer has remained brief, kept to the point, but delivered lots of pointers to tempt the reader. Note the space for putting the individual addresses in and that, again, the letter is well centred.

1 Main Street
Sometown
Newshire
AB1 CD2

Tel: 0123 57684

24th September 1997

Personnel Section
Newtown District Council
Frog Lane
Newtown
Newshire
NW1 2PP

Dear Sir or Madam,

I was very interested in your advertisement in this week's issue of
'The Mercury' for _Tourism in Newtown_ and would be grateful if
you would forward the necessary details and application form.

I look forward to hearing from you.

Yours faithfully,

ANTHEA N OTHER

Fig. 7.

1 Main Street
Sometown
Newshire
AB1 CD2

Tel: 0123 57684

24th September 1997

I would be grateful if you would accept my enclosed CV as application for the post of manager of one of your public houses. As you will see, my wife and I have a great deal of experience of both the licensed and catering trades combined with sound common sense and training in business, also teaching experience; all of which, I think, is valuable for a licensee.

My last post in the licensed trade was that of running a successful and very busy wine bar dealing with a diverse mixture of the general public and providing entertainment and food with a late licence. It was success with this position which has prompted me to approach you with the hope of running my own house.

I look forward to hearing from you.

Yours faithfully,

JOHN SMITH

Fig.8.

This letter went out to every major brewery in England, and over a dozen smaller breweries: every single one replied with an application form and every returned application form resulted in an interview. 100% success.

National Trust House

This is a case of altering one's skills to suit the vacancy (*see Fig. 9*). The writer is the same person as the previous ones but now knows that the skills need to be transferred. Also, in this type of work, age is a definite 'plus factor'. For the first time, therefore, the writer has pointed out the age in full. Also, these companies often like family women; it is not necessarily a job where promotion and ambition is high on the agenda and therefore they will look for stability, dependability above other things. The writer has emphasised these factors and is using the concept of 'Women Returners' to full advantage. Notice also that historical research is brought to the fore in this application. Instead of emphasising the 'brewery' experience, customer service is emphasised.

Shop Assistant

This is an unskilled job, with no specific vacancy in this company except that the writer noticed a massive refurbishment project underway in the county town store and realised that that would probably mean recruitment when the project was completed (*see Fig. 10*).

A word with the supervisor, (*networking*) first of all on a friendly customer basis, and then approaching the subject, meant that the writer discovered that there would be vacancies in the near future. No skills were required as they 'always train their own staff' and that the main criteria was a mature, friendly attitude. The same person altered the skills to suit.

Notice then, that the University degree is not mentioned at all. Age and maturity is emphasised in the first paragraph (as with the National Trust property). The concept of 'Woman Returner' is again brought out and this is used in the main paragraph. As is 'love of books' hinting that this is the section that the writer would prefer, as opposed to the stationery or magazine section, but is not making any demands. Notice also, that there is no mention of management experience. The writer knows that there is no vacancy at supervisory or management level and it is a completely different type of recruitment that is carried out for those posts. Also, the writer does not want to 'frighten the management away' with the idea that there might be problems over rank. The third section is a repeat of the previous letter.

Telesales

This post called upon most use of transferable skills and is therefore the longest letter (*see Fig. 11*). Note that again, reference to age is avoided - it might go against an applicant for this post. They are clearly looking for a trainee and therefore might have an eighteen year old in mind (though not necessarily).

The second paragraph is stating clearly and positively that the skills are transferable - as opposed to saying 'I do not have the skills you asked for'! It also attempts to 'butter up' the reader by referring to their excellent training policy.

Third paragraph is a rehash of the previous letters; mature, energetic self-starter- all very positive words. And now emphasising suitable aspects of the CV: - administrator, organisational ability, typing, word-processing, friendly telephone manner. Research, information, decisions, communications are emphasised here and finally, transferable skills again; the writer has done selling in the past. Again, emphasis on customer service in the final paragraph. No mention of family this time, or 'Women Returners'; this Job is for someone with energy and commitment to the company.

Targeting your letters

These posts are all very different; in terms of responsibility, career opportunities and skill-level. The applicant's priority was to secure an income not start a career and to this end was prepared to highlight certain points and play down others. There was no need to lie in any way - the same CV accompanied each letter - but it was hoped that importance would be given to the points raised in the letter.

There were also spelling mistakes in some of the letters, which shows that some errors are allowed and forgiven.

1 Main Street
Sometown
Newshire
AB1 CD2

Tel: 0123 57684

24th September 1997

Mr TJ Smith
The Director
National Trust House
Sometown
Newshire WS13 6PX

Dear Mr Smith,

I would be grateful if you would consider me for any vacancy you might have in the near future. I am mature, sensible, thirty-seven years old and, as my children are finally independent, I would like to return to full-time work.

During the years of being a full-time parent, I have enjoyed a variety of part-time or temporary work, all of which has involved dealing with the public; either in catering or licensed trades. Also, I have completed a part-time business course, specialising in tourism. My University degree is in English and History and in my final year I specialised in local historical research which makes any work at your hall of particular interest to me.

I have enclosed a CV outlining my work and education history and would be available for immediate start. I would particularly like a full-time position but would be available for temporary or part-time work.

I look forward to hearing from you.

Yours faithfully,

ANTHEA N OTHER

Fig.9.

1 Main Street
Sometown
Newshire
AB1 CD2

Tel: 0123 57684

24th September 1997

The Manager
Brilliant Books Ltd
Paper Place
Newtown
Newshire
NT7 5QP

Dear Sir or Madam

I would be grateful if you would consider me for any vacancy you might have in the near future. I am mature, sensible, thirty-seven years old and, as my children are finally independent, I would like to return to full-time work.

During the years of being a full-time parent, I have enjoyed a variety of part-time or temporary work, all of which has involved dealing with the public; either in catering or licensed trades. I have a pleasant, efficient manner and enjoy helping people in this capacity. I have a particular love of books and for this reason would especially like to work at Brilliant Books Ltd.

I have enclosed a CV outlining my work and education history and would be available for immediate start. I would particularly like a full-time position but would be available for temporary or part-time work.

I look forward to hearing from you.

Yours faithfully,

ANTHEA N OTHER

Fig.10.

1 Main Street
Sometown
Newshire
ABl CD2

Tel: 0123 57684

24th September 1997

Mr TJ Smith
Advertisement Manager
Gramsky Mercury Ltd
Gramsky House
17 Bird Street
Sometown
Newshire. WS13 6PX

Dear Mr Smith,

I was extremely interested to read of your vacancy for a Trainee Telephone Salesperson advertised in the Mercury, on 22nd September, and would be grateful if you would consider me for this position.

I have many skills which are relevant and easily transferable to this post, and I think that my enthusiasm and general education would prove a sound basis for the excellent training you offer; and that I could make a highly positive contribution to your sales team.

I am a mature, energetic and motivated self-starter with a confident attitude and outgoing personality. A sound administrator, I have good organisational skills; can type, use a word-processor and have an excellent and friendly telephone manner. A trained researcher at University, I have the ability to analyse and assimilate information quickly and to make accurate and effective decisions, even under pressure, and to communicate with people at all levels. Although many years ago, I have had experience of direct selling techniques and feel that these would be useful, especially with the benefit of more up-to-date training.

As you will see from my CV, all of my experience to date has involved working with the public at all levels, with a solid commitment to customer service and the ability to work both independently and as part of a team. I have a full driving licence, my own transport and would be available for an immediate start.

Yours sincerely,

ANTHEA N OTHER

Fig.11.

13 LAYOUT OF LETTERS

- Handwriting

Anyone who has experienced the briefest of secretarial courses will have been convinced of the importance of good layout. Those who haven't might only be aware of having red ink in the margins of their school work, or might even remember the days of having to rule in all the margins of their exercise books at school.

The rules are still there; and they can be broken, but in order to do so, you need to know what they are in the first place. Here then (*see Fig. 12*), is an example of a properly laid-out letter of application.

Ignore the actual text of the letter; the point here is the layout. The first thing to notice is that there are good margins - top and bottom, as well as left and right. I personally would leave slightly wider side margins, but that is a matter of taste.

The letter would still get an 'A' at college.

on same line of date - but this is more difficult with P.C's, so you can put it on the next line if you like.

1 Main Street
Sometown
Newshire
AB1 CD2

Tel: 0123 57684

2 line spaces here >

2 line spaces here >

24th September 1997

The Manager
Brilliant Books Ltd
Paper Place
Newtown
Newshire
NT7 5QP

3 line space here before body of letter

Dear Sir or Madam,

2 line space here

I would be grateful if you would consider me for any vacancy you might have in the near future. I am mature, sensible, thirty-seven years old and, as my children are finally independent, I would like to return to full-time work.

2 line space

During the years of being a full-time parent, I have enjoyed a variety of part-time or temporary work, all of which has involved dealing with the public; either in catering or licensed trades. I have a pleasant, efficient manner and enjoy helping people in this capacity. I have a particular love of books and for this reason would especially like to work at Brilliant Books Ltd.

2 line space

I have enclosed a CV outlining my work and education history and would be available for immediate start. I would particularly like a full-time position but would be available for temporary or part-time work.

2 line space

I look forward to hearing from you.

2 line space

Yours faithfully,

5 line space for signature to go in

ANTHEA N OTHER   *full name in capitals*

Fig.12.

Now, in between each section of information, the rule is for two lines to be left; that is, two 'enters' on the PC or carriage returns on the typewriter or imaginary lines on stationery - remember, you don't use lined paper!

After the address, date and telephone number, comes the body of the letter; that is, where you say what you want to say. Leave a slightly larger gap before you come to that; usually a three line space. This you can alter in order to create a professional finish.

At the end, the rule is for double-line spacing between the last line of your letter and 'yours sincerely' etc, and then *five* lines before your name, laid out in capital letters. This is to leave room for your signature. This also can be altered according to the length of your letter, and how the finished letter 'balances'. You can bring the last line down to balance with the first line at the top of the page. You can also bring the 'recipient's name and address' down for the same effect. This might seem to be very 'picky', but to use an example of a letter where the layout has been ignored is unimportant, see Fig. 13.

There is nothing wrong with the letter itself, except that it looks as though it has been crammed into the top of the page; and why send it out like that for the sake of a little effort to even the balance?

Mistakes *will be forgiven*, and you do not need to score lOO% on the excellence-scale every time. But if you begin with good habits, you will continue to show a high standard, so take the time to learn the correct way to produce a letter now.

Main Street
Sometown
Newshire
Personnel Section   AB1 CD2
Newtown District Council   Tel: 0123 57684
Frog Lane   24th September 1997
Newtown
Newshire
NW1 2PP

Dear Sir or Madam

I was very interested in your advertisement in this week's issue of
'The Mercury' for _Tourism in Newtown_ and would be grateful if
you would forward the necessary details and application form.

I look forward to hearing from you.

Yours faithfully,

ANTHEA N OTHER

Fig.13.

So, the *golden rules*:

- Leave good margins, top, bottom left and right.
- If hand-writing, don't slant the lines.
- Insert at top right-hand corner; your address.
- Your telephone number (leave a double line space before and after).
- The date (double line space before it).
- Next line, but against left margin:
- The recipient's name and address.

Now *three line space* and you come to the body of the letter.

- It is always best to know the name of the person to whom you are writing. Failing that, the rule is: *Dear Sir or Madam.*

I have heard it suggested that you should address your letter to 'Dear Personnel Officer' and I see this quite often these days. I would say that it would act like a red rag to a bull to someone who prizes good English and I would not recommend it at all.

These are job titles; they are not real titles such as Captain, Major, Doctor and so on, so err on the side of safety; Sir or Madam might be old fashioned, but it is still correct usage of English.

- Also, if you are addressing a woman then it is 'Ms' unless she has stated a preference herself. Don't lose your chance of a job because you have shown the boss you are sexist.

At the end comes your salutation; this is the 'Yours sincerely' or 'Yours faithfully'. The rule here is:

- *If you don't know the person* (ie if it is Dear Sir or Madam) then use Yours Faithfully.

- *If you address the person by name* (ie Dear Ms Other) then use Yours Sincerely.

Your only other decision regarding layout is whether the letter should be indented or fully-blocked. All the letters you have seen so far have been fully blocked. An example of an indented letter is shown in Fig.14.

As you can see, this is the *traditional* style of writing letters. On the address, each line is indented by a couple of spaces - and each line *always ends in a comma*, except for the last, which has the full stop.
'Dear Sir or Madam' begins against the margin, but the next line does not have line-spacing as with fully-blocked but is indented by five spaces (the average length of a word).

Then Yours sincerely/faithfully is usually centred.

With word-processing or typing, this method is more time-consuming and the 'newer' method of fully blocked is now firmly established so I doubt whether you would risk offending many people these days (ten years ago I would have advised the opposite).

1 Main Street,
Sometown,
Newshire,
HB1 CD2.

Tel: 0123 57684

24th September 1997

Personnel Section,
  Newtown District Council,
    Frog Lane,
      Newtown,
        Newshire,
          NW1 2PP.

Dear Sir or Madam,
  I was very interested in your advertisement in this week's issue of 'The Mercury' for _Tourism in Newtown_ and would be grateful if you would forward the necessary details and application form.

  I look forward to hearing from you.

Yours faithfully,

ANTHEA N OTHER

Fig.14.

Handwriting

By now, all you readers who are 'on the ball' will be muttering to yourself; 'But I thought the rule was to write letters by hand and type CVs?'

The answer to that is yes... and no. The rule has always been to hand-write your covering letter, but what about those whose handwriting is nothing short of abysmal? My handwriting is a scrawl at the best of times but, for some reason, when I want to use my 'best', it's even worse. For me to write by hand would, in all probability, reduce my chances of an interview not increase it so I type all my letters. I do still get interviews so the rule is obviously not so rigid any longer.

Another factor to take into consideration here, is the number of applications you can create in one day; with hand-writing you are seriously reducing that number. Once a letter is typed onto a word-processor you can tailor it indefinitely, taking only minutes to create new (not copied) letters to target to different employers. One client today sent out twenty speculative letters in little over an hour; I would guess that to be impossible with hand-written applications.

If you know, however, that an employer likes hand-written applications or if it specifically states that on the advertisement, then of course *only a hand-written application will do*. I know from my own experience that the more work you have to get through in a day, the more inclined you are to appreciate the typed word for, no matter how attractive a script is, it is still harder - and therefore more time-consuming - to read than a typed page.

14 APPLICATION FORMS

- Basic do's and don'ts
- Step by step to completion

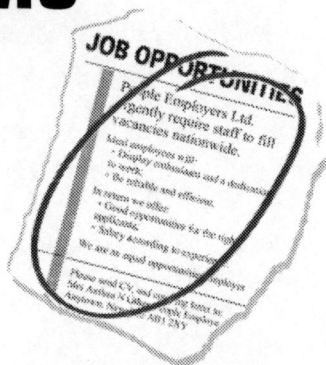

Speculative letters and standard application forms quite often go together. You spend hours writing a perfect speculative letter, enclose a CV, post it off. By return (if you're lucky) you get a reply - you think, until you open it. The envelope contains a standard application form. Now you have to spend hours transferring the information you sent on your CV to the application form - and employers never seem to send the CV back so that you can re-use it.

Basic Do's And Don'ts

- *Don't touch it!* Have it photocopied, put the master copy away. Work on the photocopy. If you make a single mistake on the master, think of it as an inch closer to that bin. They have seen thousands of that same application form filled in; and they know what a good one looks like: make sure yours is one of them.

- *Use your CV as the 'template'* for this. Refer to it; the questions will mostly be the same. The important thing is to keep the dates in order - the order that they say, that is, which will probably be 'Starting with your last Job.' - but make sure.

- *Read it thoroughly* - at least twice - before you start to answer any of the questions. Quite often, you think you know what they are referring to in a question only to find that further down the page is one more suited to the reply you gave. Not funny, especially if you then write something like 'see above' on it - that bin is looming closer.

- *Read any instructions carefully.* I would suggest using black ink from now on to avoid any errors in later forms because increasingly it will say, in small print, *use black ink only* and if you don't, they can't photocopy it and your form is wasted.

- *Technically, you can use a typewriter* but a) I have never managed to use one to fill in a form successfully and b) I have never heard an employer say he actually prefers them typewritten. The closest I have heard is a personnel officer saying, 'We won't hold it against her, but...'

- I think of these forms in the same way as a driving test; you won't fail if you make one mistake. They can mount up and how many you will be allowed will depend on the person receiving it and how bad he thinks the mistake is.

- *Make sure you answer every question.* Don't leave any blank spaces in your work history and don't leave any answer boxes unanswered. They know what they are asking and why; they want that answer. Don't write 'Refer to answer above' - that seems to be lethal!

Remember: any employer *wants to give you the job*. If they can do that, their search is over; they want to have a full work force. The job is there for you if you say and do the right thing. The right thing, of course, is giving them what they are looking for. That is not so mysterious as it seems - or as mysterious as I thought it was when I was looking for work. They want someone who is honest, reliable, who won't leave as soon as they have trained them, who will fit in - won't cause waves - and who they can depend on. You are all of those things. Just be yourself... but neatly, tidily, efficiently...using black ink.

Show your skills

The task for the employer is to see if the information on your application form matches up to the Job specifications. Therefore, you should always make a conscious effort to show this as you fill it in. With a letter you can say what transferable skills you have; with an application form, you must show it.

Many personnel officers sift through these applications with a 'tick sheet' next to them. If the job specification calls for numeracy, good typing skills, high energy and sense of humour, then those words are the ones which will be on the sheet. You won't get a 'tick' for anything else; that's what they will be looking for.

It is important to keep the form tidy, the lines straight, and the information in relevant sections. If you really do want this job, it is the only way to proceed and you must spend time on it. After the employer has sifted through and discarded those who are hopelessly off-target, his next job will be to try to build up a picture of the remaining applicants.

Personal matters

Application forms do vary tremendously these days; some can be extremely intrusive and there are several that I have refused to fill in on these grounds. Some questions, however, are not so intrusive as they might appear. For instance, some companies ask about your family background. The main reason for this seems to be so they can judge whether or not you are an achiever. If you have two A levels and you say so on the form that is all it means. There is little other information that goes with it from which the reader can build a picture.

However, add these two A levels to your family background and the story changes completely. If you come from a background of financial and intellectual poverty, those two A levels are indeed an achievement and therefore say a great deal about you.

The picture can build up further by matching up the years in which you studied for the A levels with those years in your work history.

For instance, during 1984-86, you passed two A level exams. In the employment history column, it says you were working for a haulage company as a long-distance lorry driver. Did you therefore turn those hours when you were parked up overnight into positive use by studying? If your hobbies column then says that you coached a school football team at weekends, and that you have a young family, this all adds up to someone who is industrious, energetic, committed and thoughtful.

Now add this picture to what you know of family background; parents are both unskilled factory workers?

Well this applicant has moved on several notches from his own beginnings; with the right opportunity, he could go far. His method of progression is slower because of his family commitments. If the current vacancy is for an administrator in a haulage company, then the reason for the application is obvious; progression. The new skills can be learned as has been proved by the A levels.

But if this same applicant has a father who is a University lecturer and mother is primary school head-mistress? If, in the employment category, 1984-86 is blank and the applicant has no family commitments? Two A levels then is not much to say for two years, is it?

Step By Step To Completion

So! You have your application form, your photocopies of it. You have your job description which you have read at least a couple of times and which you have highlighted for relevant important points.

- Now you need your own CV, your skills sheets, and a list of good, positive words.

- Before you start on your photocopies, go through this job description jotting down those requirements which you have proven relevant experience for; i.e. those specific skills which you have used in the same type of work.

- Now look for the requirements for which you can use transferable skills. Write all of them down, because later you want to combine them or to sift out those which look best.

- Read between the lines of the Job description and compare your own personality with it. What kind of person are they looking for? Now list those aspects of your personality which favour these descriptions. If all your hobbies and interests, for instance, take place with lots of people and all your previous jobs have been high-profile, public orientated, applying for a job as lorry driver is going to look odd, isn't it?

- If you are sure that is what you want and it is not a whim brought on by a fit of pique with the boss or underlying depression, then you must explain this change of aim and be convincing otherwise, again, the questions will remain.

- There is almost always a section on an application form where you can list other information. This often takes the shape of; 'Anything else which can support your application' or, 'Why do you think you are the best person for this Job?'

- The second question is quite specific and needs careful thought but the point is obvious. It is your chance to show that you know what the job entails and that you know about the company, its policies; and all your transferable skills, aims, ambitions can be made clear in this section. Make good use of the space. Take a lot of time to think about it; preferably seek a second opinion, which is always beneficial.

- The other, open kind of question, is more difficult and depends on the individual application. You must use this if your skills are mainly transferable; take time to point out all your qualities which are right for this job.

- Unfortunately, by the time you get to this section, which is usually at the end, you can already feel jaded from all the preparation and hard work you have put in so far. It is a good idea to leave this for a while. Mull it over while you do other things and go back to it later when you are feeling fresh. It is important, it will be read, and the employer will be looking at everything carefully.

Now check your notes through carefully. There will almost certainly be waffle at this stage, so cross it all out. If you have used long-winded sentences, shorten them by using more precise words.

- Are your explanations for leaving previous jobs acceptable?

- Make sure they are.

- *Don't lie!* But make sure that everything is shown in its best light and remember that you will be questioned further in your interview.

Always keep in mind the job you are applying for when you write in your Job Description column. For instance, if you have a career history in the hotel and catering trade, and you are now applying for a pub management position; is there a catering element to the new post? If not, then you are wasting time highlighting the catering aspect of your background; you might even put them off if they know they are never going to be able to make use of those skills. Highlight the bar side of your experience - the cellar work, the real ales, and so on.

On the subject of pubs - leisure interests should look good; don't give them any cause to wonder if you are going to be turning up with a hang-over or taking unexplained, extra-long lunch breaks.

The Personnel Officer's role

Applications will be sifted into three categories; those which are definite non-starters will go into the 'rejected' pile.

Those which offer all the requirements, so they go into the 'interview' pile. Then there is the middle-ground, the grey area. This will comprise those applications which seem to fulfil most of the criteria but who have fallen short on one or two things. Perhaps the overall look of the application is not as neat as it could have been; lots of crossings-out and spelling mistakes, but the content itself seems good. The employer would then be worried about not interviewing this person in case there was some good reason for the messy application form; and he might then miss out on a good worker.

The grey area

The risk you take with this is a) it is already in the employer's mind that your submission is not all it could have been. He will be reminded of this when you enter the interview because he will have your form in front of him. b) what if he has received ten excellent applications, and six 'middle-grounds' - and he only wants to interview a dozen people? You would never know if that is what had happened because you will just receive the same rejection letter as the original non-starters.

You must bear in mind at all times that, if you are responding to an advertised vacancy, there could be two hundred other applicants. They have to be sifted down to a manageable proportion - and I would say that proportion would be a maximum of a dozen. Get used to that image of the 200-pile and that 190-bin.

15 SPECULATIVE PHONECALLS

- Prepare for action

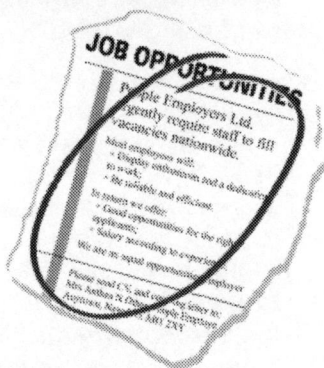

Okay, so you want to make phone calls; you think it will be quicker, overall cheaper, and you will know where you stand sooner. But you don't know what to say, do you? Well, if you do, then you don't want any help from me. I've heard calls that I thought couldn't possibly get anything and which have resulted in an interview; and textbook perfect calls go down like the proverbial lead balloon. The one good thing is that if it is going to fail, at least it does so quickly and you can move on to the next one.

Prepare For Action

There are some really obvious do's and don'ts which I hope you already use:

- *Pen and Paper* - Don't even touch the phone unless you have a pen and notepad in front of you.

- *Try to be efficient;* if you are going to ring a dozen companies at once it is better to have just one address and number in front of you at a time or you are likely (as I did once to my intense embarrassment) to forget who you are talking to and say the wrong thing.

- *Try to know who you are going to speak to,* and ask for them by name. If you can't find out then ask if there is a personnel or recruitment department (or officer). That will get you through. There is nothing more off-putting than rehearsing your words, getting through, giving your blurb to be responded to by, 'One moment; I'll put you through.' Silence. 'Hello?' You say the whole thing over again and it's followed by, 'Um, I think you've been put through to the wrong department; I'll put you back to switch-board.' Sometimes it can actually break the ice, cause a laugh with the person on the other end but just as often it leads to frustration - and if you are paying for the call (which I've told you not to!)...

- *Try to speak clearly.* If you have a strong accent, it doesn't matter; if it is a local one, perhaps the operator has the same. What does matter is that if you slur the words and she can't understand you, you will embarrass her, make her feel irritated that she has to keep saying pardon. In the end, she won't even bother trying to write down what you are saying - it costs her nothing to lose your call.

- For the same reason as above, *be polite.*

What are you ringing for?

This might not be so obvious as it seems, especially if you are calling a large company. They have hundreds of employees in dozens of categories; do you want the job as caretaker, secretary to the director, director? Do you want to be their liaison officer, their accountant, their labourer? The subject is so wide I can't answer this for you or even give you any examples; if you want a specific job, then simply state what you are looking for, like this:

'Hello, my name is John Smith. I'm calling to enquire if you have any vacancies for shop-floor worker, or if you might have any in the near future.'

'No. I'm sorry, we've no vacancies at the moment.'

'Do you know if you'll be recruiting in the near future?'

'Not a mass recruitment, but we do get occasional vacancies. I can't say.'

'Could you tell me the best way to make a speculative approach?'

'Yes, you can send your CV in; it will be kept on file.'

Don't leave it there; she's being helpful!

'Could you tell me how you normally recruit - is it through the local press, or the Job Centre?'

'We do use the press and Job Centre if it's for more than one vacancy; but often we recruit for a single vacancy through our waiting list. What kind of work have you done before?'

Bingo! This kind of positive call does happen - and when it does, are you spurred on! You haven't got a job; you haven't even found a vacancy; but that person was nice; you used a method that worked; you caused her to be nice to you; you were in control and you succeeded. This is the kind of thing that makes you hooked on the telephone and thankful that you're not paying for the calls... are you?

Follow up right away

When this happens, don't lose time: *send your CV and covering letter immediately*. Also, in the covering letter, refer to the call: 'You might remember I spoke with you yesterday/today concerning possible vacancies and I would therefore...'

You did ask the speaker her name before you hung up, didn't you: and you did ask for the correct address and department to send your application to? *Didn't you?* If you didn't, you're no worse than me and a million others; kick yourself and phone the switchboard back - ask them - don't ask to be put through to that Very Important Person again. You don't want her to think you're a dolt. Besides, if the girl on the switchboard sounds nice, you can tell her you're an idiot; tell her what you've done (or not done, rather) and you can laugh together - that way she will remember you and that is always good. She might even have a joke about it with the personnel officer - and that is brilliant.

If she's not friendly, don't even think about it; you'll only get a frosty response, lose your confidence and waste your time.

Whatever happens: post that CV today.

You can do this indefinitely. Have your Yellow Pages, Thomson Directory, whatever you are using today. Keep calling as long as you feel confident because it shows through in your voice and nothing breeds success like success.

16 INTERVIEWS

- Fear of failure
- Practical aspects of interviews
- Interview them too

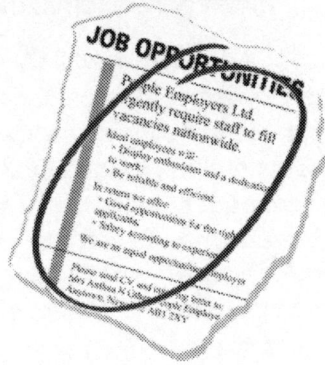

Interviews. You either love them or hate them; rise to the challenge or wilt under the prospect. And sometimes both at different times in your life.

The more you like them, see them as a challenge, feel excited rather than intimidated by them, then the better you are likely to do. It doesn't have to be that way and an interviewer will not always see the person who is most relaxed, casual, etc, in a positive light - especially if the interviewer himself was one of those poor, nervous wretches who came out in a cold sweat at the very thought of an interview. He might think you are arrogant or that you do not view him with the due amount of respect.

Added to this, in research, interviews have never been shown to be an accurate way of judging the right person for a job. Despite increasingly sophisticated methods of carrying out these interviews and training the interviewer, the results have still not shown them to be reliable. One suggestion is that the decision about you is made in the first few minutes and the rest of the time is just spent endorsing that original opinion of the interviewer. Not much pleasure in that if your interview took two hours and you didn't get the job at the end of it.

Good interviewers will try not to let this happen; they will acknowledge their prejudices which were at work in the first few minutes. But allow for what you say and do in the following time to influence your decision - and take account of the amount of stress you might be feeling. Research has shown that even this can be biased - either for or against you, it should be added! It could be that in the first minute of meeting, the interviewer decided you are the very person he wants to fill that vacancy; do you then feel so strongly against their selection procedures?

Interviews are all very different, run according to the company's own policy - or lack of one. They can all be predicted within certain parameters; you are always going to be asked about your work history, they are always going to encourage you to talk about yourself. They will always look for any worrying signs that you might not fit in or cause them problems later.

Any person who has had the unpleasant task of having to fire someone is going to be much more careful about their initial choice in future.

If you have researched interview techniques then you should know within a few minutes what kind of interview you are in. You will therefore have a better idea of what is to follow.

On the other hand, you walk into the room and find it is the MD's office, that it is stuffed to the gills with unfiled papers, indecipherable wall charts and constantly ringing telephone. You know for sure this is a chaotic environment and probably a boss who does not delegate. If he offers you a drink, then you know at least that he has manners and might be quite pleasant to work for; but do you want the chaos?

But to be in this situation of being able to forecast how an interview is going to be conducted, then you must first of all have done your research. You should know the various methods of interviewing.

I would suggest that you spend as much time as possible on this aspect of your job search. Like everything else we have looked at so far, the more preparation you have put in beforehand the better able you are to cope, and the stronger your confidence will be. When I had my last interview I was very rusty - it was my first interview in several years and I struggled throughout.

My one overriding feeling as I was driving home was that if I had known what it would be like I would have done so much better. That is, if I'd had another to go to the following day, I'm sure I would have excelled.

Well, there are two lessons to be learnt from this; one is, I hadn't done my homework and I should have. The second point is, it is much better to line your interviews up if you can. Don't arrange one interview if you can arrange half a dozen. Your techniques become better and more relaxed with practice.

Fear Of Failure

Be honest with yourself; if you are 'looking for work' but never seem to get the offers of interviews, are you sure you're not secretly conspiring with yourself because you are scared of the possibility of failure? Are you in some way ensuring you don't get the interviews? Or, perhaps you get the interviews, but don't turn up - realising at the last minute that 'it's not really the right job' or 'I'd have problems with transport,' location, whatever..?

If this has been happening to you and you sense fear is at the root of it, you can get help. Any of the courses I have mentioned will offer you interview techniques and mock interview situations. There are private consultancies and careers services which specialise in these areas if you are able to pay. Quite often, the main problem is that you have become socially isolated. The fear then of being suddenly confronted with a group of strangers all assessing you, judging you, is very real. The simple act of enrolling on one of these courses will get you 'out of yourself', increase your self-esteem and bring back your old yearning for challenge. If it doesn't, that is still not a problem; it simply means that your 'hang-up' or insecurity is lying deeper than the course leaders have touched on. Or they haven't quite provided the answer; don't give up, simply continue your research, ask for another course, seek out the answers!

Again, the longer you have been out of work, the deeper these new habits will have embedded themselves. And that is all they are *new habits*; easy to wipe out. You think you are a failure, that you have nothing to offer any longer, that your skills are outdated, useless, your education is insufficient, non-existent; that you have lost all you ever had. Let me tell you now, one week in a new job and your confidence will be soaring just like it was in the old days, you'll be walking straighter, smiling easier, laughing again. Try to keep hold of that image, because you can act like you feel that way already; and that will stand you in good stead both for the interviews to come and your choice of target.

Aim beyond your present capabilities

Anyone who has bought a house must remember those first weeks after signing the mortgage agreement. Do you remember thinking you would never be able to keep up the payments? Yet two years later, how did you feel about those same payments? If you are like most people, you had simply got used to them. I suggest you make your job targets like that; if you strive for something you are sure you can do now then you are striving too low. In a few weeks, let alone months, it will be beneath your level of expertise. You will be bored and, I promise you, you will wish you had strived just a little bit harder.

Look for work that is just out of reach. Perhaps you can do sixty, seventy percent of it, but you know that there are aspects that you don't know, that you will have to learn. That is about the right level and any company who recognises skill will think the same. They won't want you to know everything, because they will fear you will become bored and want to move on. This will not be a problem with the interview; don't feel you will have to bluff your way in. Concentrate, remind yourself about the sixty percent you do know and be confident about your ability to learn the other forty per cent.

Practical Aspects Of Interviews

Prepare beforehand

There are some things you simply must do in order to prepare for interviews. The first and most obvious thing is to be on time. For that, you need to back track on all the things you need to do in order to ensure your arrival is on time. These are obvious but many people fall down on them, including myself in one very embarrassing circumstance; did I do it deliberately because I was so afraid?

If you are able to, then it is always a good idea to have a 'dummy run'; time the journey, find out precisely where the interview is taking place, where the parking is, the public transport, the nearest cafe if you are going to arrive too early and so on. All these things will help your nerves and confidence when the time comes.

Know the company

Find out as much as you can about the company. That is essential; whatever level you are being interviewed for. Know as much as you can about the type of job you are applying for, and how it works in that particular company. You can sometimes bluff your way with this, but it isn't good for your confidence again.

Know yourself

And especially what you said to them! If you conducted your job search properly you will have a copy of the letter, the CV, the application form; everything that you have said to them so far. Keep them with you, read them the night before, perhaps also take extra copies of your CV with you in case it is a panel interview and they only have one copy between them. That way you can show both your thoughtfulness and your efficiency by offering them a copy each. But beware that you don't underline their own inefficiency by doing this.

First impressions

First impressions do count. The thing to do is try to minimise those things that can work against you. Bad habits and mannerisms are high on the list here; tapping your fingers loudly on a chair would be a definite cross against you! Inappropriate behaviour - laughing or cracking jokes loudly when no-one is even smiling might not go down too well. Striding in, picking up a chair, moving it to where you want it to be... you are taking over the show; and on someone else's territory, when they think you should be presenting a suitably submissive front.

Things like this make life easy for the interviewer; they can simply cross you off their selection list and wind down the interview. They are easy for you too; you know not to do these things. But these 'over-the-top' actions apart, there is a very subtle grey area of what is right, wrong, good and bad in interviews. Some you can help yourself, by practising, rehearsing, good preparation. Others will be destined for that first few minutes' appraisal which is down to the interviewer's personal, subjective likes and dislikes which you can have no prior knowledge of and so in that sense you can do no more and no better than to just be yourself.

Grand entrance

Don't forget that an interviewer knows that you are on your way. Many make a point of taking a 'quick peep' at the interviewee before their actual introduction. I would say that your interview starts the moment you leave your home and set out on your journey; are you sure that that person you just sounded your horn at and made that nasty gesture to isn't your prospective new boss?

You are very definitely being interviewed the moment you enter their building, whoever sees you, or whoever you make enquiries from. Rehearse your big entrance on them. Smile, be polite, show charm and consideration; it can't do you any harm and the lack of it certainly could.

Walking in

The moment has arrived. Even if you have been kept waiting, if you are not impressed with the manners or protocol they have shown so far, don't show it. This is your moment; if they fall short, you don't have to.

Don't rush; don't show panic at the final moment. Walk in, smiling! Keep anything you are carrying in your left hand in case they want to shake hands. Always respond with a good firm handshake but don't offer yours first. Let them take the lead. Go to the chair but don't sit until they offer it. It is their place to welcome you so don't thwart them of their right to show manners to you.

Mannerisms

It is best to keep these under control. Nail biting, excessive movement - bobbing about in your chair - fidgeting and waving your arms around, are all signs of nervousness and most of us do some of these things. When we are concentrating on what we are saying and in a state of nervousness, it is easy to forget about them and irritate the life out of a stranger. So try to get into the habit of not doing it. One solution is to carry your clip-board with your CV and letter. That way it stops you from waving your arms about too much (and sending that mug of coffee flying over the boss' suit!).

Introductions

Even if you are hopeless at remembering names, do make a special effort now. I am the last person to talk about this because in the initial moments nothing sinks into my brain at all; and that's usually the time you are told their names. Just because I'm beyond help doesn't mean you have to be. At least recognise the importance and that it does go in your favour if you can call them by name.

Posture

Nothing goes down so well as enthusiasm and slouching in your chair will give precisely the opposite message. By the same token, don't sit rigidly to attention either; you will simply look terrified and make everyone feel uncomfortable. Think of Mastermind; set yourself comfortably in that chair, look relaxed, alert, and friendly. Even if you don't feel any of these things at the moment - acting it is half way to being it. The general consensus is to sit straight, lean slightly forward and, above all, make eye contact.

Smile

My personal opinion is that this is the most important thing of all, perhaps with eye contact coming as a close second. The very fact that you have been invited to interview means that they have accepted your CV - even if with reservations or subject to questions, but nevertheless, on paper, you are acceptable.

By definition, therefore, your personality is the thing that is being questioned here. They want to like you. A good smile might not make them instantly fall in love; but I suspect the complete lack of one will instantly deflate them and cause rejection. Even a nervous smile is okay; they know you're going to be nervous; they expect it; they are prepared to work to put you at your ease. Don't let them down by giving them unpleasant surprises.

Dress

Be prepared physically. That means make sure your clothes are appropriate, that you are presenting a suitable image. I would suggest that to deliberately not do so means that you are telling them quite explicitly that you do not want the job. There is also the factor that you could be sabotaging your own chances. Some people become so stressed by interviews that they make inappropriate decisions at this stage.

Quiet is smart

This is the guideline I would use. Obviously, there are exceptions, but those you will know about and alter yourself accordingly. And remember, dressing for the interview is not the same as dressing for the job. Social workers in an outward bound centre might normally wear baggy jeans and sloppy sweaters, but when you go before the board of a county council interview I cannot visualise the patched jeans winning any votes.

The cold shoulder

If they are game-players and part of the 'dirty tricks brigade', they might sit, uninvitingly po-faced, with two empty chairs and not even offer one to you. Well, you know what you are dealing with when this happens; don't let their bad manners reduce yours.

I have a friend who attended an interview with a particularly prestigious regiment of the armed forces. When he entered he found a large imposing room with a long,

long walk to the panel of unsmiling faces. A few steps in he realised there was no chair for him. As he looked back, the chair was behind the door.

He retraced his steps, picked up the chair and walked with it to the panel of interviewers, placed it where it should have been in the first place and introduced himself. They did not react to his action. They proceeded with what he described as an interrogation.

Imagine his astonishment when they later informed him that he had been accepted into the regiment. The commission which he had worked towards for a long time had turned sour for him and he rejected the offer. They then demanded his presence to explain himself! They obviously considered their arrogance justified but he did not. In his words, they had 'failed the interview'.

Interview Them Too

Any company worth its salt should be careful of its own image. If they interview eleven people for each vacancy, then there are ten people who leave who have personal knowledge of their behaviour. To go against your better judgement after an interview; to accept the post simply on the grounds that you have been offered it, can be storing up trouble for yourself.

It is very difficult to turn down a job after it has been offered, particularly if you have financial pressures, have been out of work for a long time and are feeling desperate.

My own experience tells me 'better now than later'. I have heard people recommend that you take the job anyway because you can always look for something else. It is true that it seems easier to find work when you are in work; that is, that employers are sometimes biased against people who have been unemployed for a long time.

If you really feel that you would be a square peg trying to squeeze into a round hole then no matter how hard you try, you will continue to be battling against a constant fear of failure.

Moreover, as you continue with your job search, you then have the added problem of what to tell prospective employers; admit that you only took the job till you could find something better? I don't think that would go down well with anyone! Your present company is not going to like you for wasting their time and resources and what kind of reference do you think they'll give?

I know someone who seemed to have a complete personality change through finding himself in this position. He had not been unemployed in the first place, simply thought that it was time for a career move.

He interviewed, accepted the new post, and then found that he just did not fit in. He did not share their values and nor did he want to. He said, after some months, that he had reached the stage where he saw all his commitments as being millstones pinning him down; if he did not own his house he would have no need to suffer the job; if he did not have hobbies, then he would not need it, and so on; every aspect of his life became tainted.

Worse, he said, because he was in a profession it was

impossible for him to make a move before two years. To do so would either make him look unstable, or make it seem as if he were rubbishing the profession as a whole: he was stuck.

17 AND FINALLY..

- Be organised

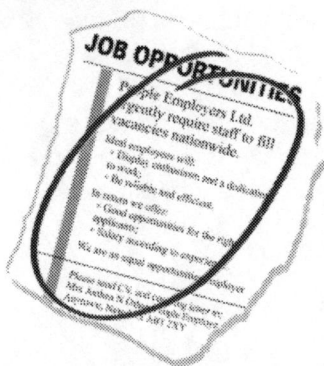

You have stuck through to the end; that deserves congratulations in itself. If you have completed the exercises and followed up on advice I have given; visited the various centres, perhaps read other books, then you are a winner. *Every person I have ever encountered who has done this has achieved their own aims!*

Be Organised

There only remains the tidying up now. You will start your job search but it won't always work in sequence; you might send a letter of application today but find that you have to attend an interview tomorrow for a job you applied for a month ago; and tomorrow you might receive an application form for another. If you are applying for many jobs, this is the way it will work and you need to be organised in your methods.

You could well find yourself highlighting your qualifications at an interview where you had previously decided to play these down. Some people are naturally tidy and organised; I'm not, alas, so have learned the hard way that these things must be done. Keep a record of *every* company you contact, even if it is only a speculative phone call, write it down.

Keep a log:

- the company
- the address
- the telephone number
- the person you spoke to
- the department you were put through to
- that person's name,
- and the result.

I wasn't always this organised and it was incredibly frustrating and expensive having to track down that number again. If you don't keep track of them you will lose good contacts.

When you receive a letter inviting you to interview, do confirm it. It should be by letter really, but these days companies seem to prefer the speed of the telephone; but you could phone and then follow up with a short note. It

shouldn't be a long letter; just thank them for their letter/
call and say that you will be happy to attend interview at
the given time and place. Do write the time and place out
specifically because if there has been a mistake, it can be
corrected.

Many people also follow up their interviews with a courtesy
letter thanking the interviewer for their time and
consideration. It all depends on how keen you are on letter
writing; I don't think it would change a person's mind
about whether to offer you the job or not; but if they have
already decided in your favour it can start you off on a
specially-good footing.

It can also be a good idea to write a note of thanks to
someone when they have just written to tell you they have
no jobs. Thank them for their trouble and tell them that
you are still interested and would they mind keeping you
on file. I think this is the most profitable one of all, as it
shows your interest and reminds them of you. Also, you
can follow this through with a little reminder in a month or
so.

But you can only do this with an accurate log.

Believe me, after you have sent out forty applications you
will not be able to remember who you have written to or
what you said to them. You really should aim for that
figure every week if you want maximum feedback. One
researcher found that it takes around fifty applications to
find work. If that is so, better get the numbers out in a
week rather than six months!

Keep yourself 'polished'; perfect your skills, work on them

and don't lose sight of your goals. Above all, when you feel yourself becoming jaded, *stop*; take a rest, have a couple of days off. In work you would do this and from now on, think of finding work as being a full-time job. You might not have found a job this week but you have worked hard at it; you deserve your time off. Enjoy your weekend!

I was very lucky when I was a member of Jobclub in that the leader recognised this aspect and she would notice when someone was becoming despondent. She would change the subject away from work, motivate them about their hobbies or other interests and then send them away refreshed. Do this for yourself; the very fact that you have read this book, carried out the immense effort in following these exercises means that you are committed to your task. You are working hard; *you will succeed.*

HELP LIST

- Further reading
- Helpful contacts

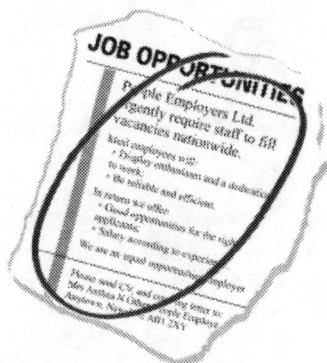

How to Start a Career

Judith Johnstone, pub.
How To Books Ltd, 1994

Women Mean Business

Ed, Caroline Bamford &
Catherine McCarthy, pub.
BBC Books, 1991

Psychological Testing for Managers

Stephanie Jones, pub.
Piatkus 1993

Succeed at your Job Interview

George Heaviside, pub.
BBC Books 1993

How to Face Interviews

Clive Fletcher, pub.
Thorsons 1986

Coping with Stress at Work

Jacqueline Matkinson Phd,
pub. Thorsons 1988

Assertiveness at Work

Ken Black and Kate Black,
pub. McGraw-Hill Book
Company 1992

Women Returners Guide

Linda Stoker, pub.
Bloomsbury 1991

CVs and Written Applications

Judy Skeats

Getting the Right Job

Judy Skeats

Returning to Work: A Practical Guide for Women

Alec Reed, pub Kogan Page, 1989

Hiring and Firing: Employing and Managing People

Karen Lanz, Nat West Small Business Bookshelf 1988

Presenting Yourself

(for women) Mary Spillane, Piatkus 1993

The Perfect CV

Tom Jackson, Piatkus 1991

Writing Effective Letters and Memos

A. H. Bell & Cherie Kester, Cassell 1991

Writing

Catherine Hilton & Margaret Hyder, Letts Educational 1992

Contacts

For this subject, information is freely and easily obtainable.

The best places to start are;

- Your local Job Centre
- Local library
- County H.Q. libraries have masses of information!
- A careers advisor - but ask first if there is a charge

Career Analysts

Career House, 90 Gloucester Place, London W1H 4BL.

Ask for details of what they offer.

National Organisation for Women's Management

132 Abbey Road, London, NW6 6SN - Contact Dorothy Badrick.

Women Returners Network

Garden Cottage,
Youngsbury, Ware, Herts.
SG13 0TZ

Tel: 01920 464337

Careers for Women

4th Floor, 2 Valentine
Place, London SEl 8QH.

Tel: 0171 4012280 -
answers questions on
careers by post.

The World's Your Oyster
Education and Training for Adults
Polly Bird ISBN 1-86144-014-6
£5.99 110pp Pub July 96

A complete guide to education and training for adults.
The number of mature entrants to higher education in the
UK in 1993 was up by 128% on 1982.

Stress-Busting
The Essential Guide To Staying In Control
Nick Daws ISBN 1-86144-027-8
£5.99 118pp Pub Jan 97

Stress has been described as the twentieth century disease.
Contrary to the popular stereotype, the ulcer-ridden
businessman popping pills as he makes multi-million
pound decisions is only a small part of the picture. You
can just as easily suffer from stress if you are a
housewife...a factory worker...a civil servant...a driver...a
police officer...a student.
Whatever your background, if stress is making your life a
misery, help is at hand.

Education Matters

Professional Advice for Parents
David Abbott ISBN 1-86144-029-4
£6.99 128pp Pub July 97

Your child can become a winner in the education stakes. A teacher tells you how.
If you've ever felt confused by schools or curriculum, don't be. David Abbott cuts through ther jargon to make sense of education. You'll know your way around, and feel confident making the smart moves to get the best education for your child.

The Facts About the Menopause

Coping Before, During and After
Elliot Philipp ISBN 1-86144-034-0
£6.99 100pp Pub Oct 97

The menopause signifies a new period in a woman's life. It is usually a time of less responsibilities at home and at work and the time when the nuisance of monthly periods stops. It should be a time of freedom to do many things that are fulfilling and satisfying. This book describes in detail the many symptoms that may be experienced, shows their causes and possible treatments. It helps prepare the body and mind for a healthy laterlife.

Need2Know

Thank you for buying one of our books. We hope you found it an enjoyable read and useful guide. Need2Know produce a wide range of informative guides for people in difficult situations. Available in all good bookshops, or alternatively direct from:

Need2Know
1-2 Wainman Road
Woodston
Peterborough
PE2 7BU
Order Hotline: 01733 238140
Fax: 01733 230751

Titles

____	**Buying A House**	£5.99
____	**Stretch Your Money**	£4.99
____	**Breaking Up**	£5.99
____	**Superwoman**	£4.99
____	**Work For Yourself And Win**	£5.99
____	**The Expatriate Experience**	£6.99
____	**You And Your Tenancy**	£5.99
____	**Improving Your Lifestyle**	£5.99
____	**Safe As Houses**	£5.99
____	**The World's Your Oyster**	£5.99
____	**Everything You Need2Know About Sex**	£5.99
____	**Travel Without Tears**	£5.99
____	**Prime Time Mothers**	£5.99
____	**Parenting Teenagers**	£5.99